"It's a safe bet that 'The Donald' won't h[...] instigated by this book. And there's the p[...]. Donald's not big on church and has heard few sermons in his lifetime. However, some of the folks who put their trust in Trump may attend to sermons and therefore may be urged to think like Christians about the age in which we live. I love Wes Allen's conviction that the elevation of Trump is a call for better preaching. Our national mistake, when viewed through the eyes of faith, is great opportunity to reflect more engagingly upon the gospel. If you are a preacher, wondering what to say in the Age of Trump (and I hope you are) this book is a godsend. Thanks, Wes."

— Will Willimon, Duke Divinity School, United Methodist Bishop (retired), and Author of *Who Lynched Willie Earle?*

"Preaching in the Age of Trump is like a much-needed urgent care facility for preachers reeling from the election and its aftermath. Wes Allen not only offers an accurate diagnosis for how our country and the church have found themselves in this place of crisis, but prescribes effective strategies for preachers to address the fear, turmoil, prejudices, hatred, and divisiveness of this time, as well as the need for proclaiming prophetic justice. While never mincing words about the staggering array of evil now before us, Allen also reminds us in this must-have book that the preacher's task is to address the humanity of our congregations, even while casting out the demonic forces that hold us in thrall."

— Leah D. Schade, Lexington Theological Seminary, Author of *Creation-Crisis Preaching*

"President Donald J. Trump has ushered in a new era of post-truth, alternative facts, and intimidation tactics targeting everyone from the intelligence community to national media. His tweets spew racism, hate, and intolerance, and his orders have separated families, desecrated tribal lands, and closed America's doors to the refugee. These harrowing times demand that the prophetic voice of the pulpit arise and resist. Dr. Allen has masterfully and insightfully provided a way forward to accomplish this."

— Michael W. Waters, Joy Tabernacle A.M.E. Church in Dallas, Author of *Stakes Is High*

"It would be hard to imagine a more timely or important book. As the church awakens to the reality of fascism at home and abroad, the prophetic timidity of mainline clergy must bear some of the blame. Preachers have been sleeping through history, our voices muzzled by phony arguments about politics in the pulpit and faith as a purely individual affair. Wes Allen has made it clear that now is the time to clear our throats and speak truth to power again. Let's hope we are not too late. If we are, let's go down preaching."

— Robin R. Meyers, Mayflower UCC Church in Oklahoma City, Author of *Spiritual Defiance*

"Wes Allen has written a timely and important book that addresses one of the fundamental questions the church faces in what feels like a cultural crossroads: How do we preach faithfully in a world where so many congregations are divided over the issue of a Donald Trump presidency? Walking a fine line between the pastoral and the prophetic, Allen offers practical wisdom sure to challenge all preachers in search of authentic ways to navigate these uncertain times. This is a book all preachers need right now."

— Derek Penwell, Douglass Boulevard Christian Church in Louisville, Author of *The Mainliner's Survival Guide to the Post-Denominational World*

"All preaching is contextual. All preaching has its own urgency. All preaching is the interaction of people with one another. All preaching matters. There are times when these realities seem to be in vivid color—almost surreal color. Many of us feel that the age of Trump has put an 'Instagram-like filter' on our context, urgency, and interactions so that it matters all the more what we say and how we say it. Many of us recognize that something has to change, that something has changed. Wes Allen's insights, passion, and pastoral heart are what so many of us need at this time. This book's modern-day 'pastoral epistle feel' makes this a book we need. And we need the kinds of preaching Allen calls for."

— Doug Pagitt, Solomon's Porch in Minneapolis, Author of *Preaching Reimagined*

"Many ministers are struggling with how to proclaim the gospel of Christ in congregations polarized by partisan politics, racial tensions, and fake news. O. Wesley Allen Jr. takes on the challenge of how to not only give voice to the gospel but also relate it to the world outside the church walls. Allen's examination and clarity of several homiletical strategies crossing a wide range of pertinent issues and policy decisions will help ministers and the Church respond to the widening rift in our society and congregations with meaningful, Christ-centered conversations."

— Evan M. Dolive, Author of *Seeking Imperfection: Body Image, Marketing and God*

For my daughter Maggie:
your passion for social justice is contagious
and has served as an inspiration for this work.

PREACHING
in the ERA *of*

O. Wesley Allen Jr.

chalice
press
Saint Louis, Missouri

An imprint of Christian Board of Publication

Bible quotations, unless otherwise marked, are from the *New Revised Standard Version Bible,* copyright 1989, Division of Christian Education of the National Council of the Churches of Christ in the United States of America. Used by permission. All rights reserved.

Cover design: Lynne Condellone

ChalicePress.com

Print: 9780827231481
EPUB: 9780827231498   EPDF: 9780827231504

Printed in the United States of America

Contents

INTRODUCTION

On November 10, 2016, the day after Donald Trump was elected, I received and initiated texts, phone calls, and emails with friends and colleagues in ministry. One layperson said, "As a Christian, I don't understand how anyone voted for him. Church didn't prepare me for this." Clergy friends raised the question over and over again: "What in the world am I going to say on Sunday?" After one of the most negative campaigns in recent history resulting in a president-elect many fear will reinstitutionalize bigotry and oppression, how does one offer God's good news?

This book aims to join the conversation struggling with that question. To be honest, I had not even thought of entering this fray until my friend Ron Allen pushed me in this direction. He certainly would have done a better job than I, but I appreciate his confidence in passing the buck to me. I was reluctant to pick up this mantle, but my wife and daughter...well...*insisted.* These two women had been so excited about the possibility of having one of their own finally preside from the Oval Office, and felt their hearts had been plucked out of their chests—not just when a man beat Hillary Clinton in a surprise victory—but when this *particular* sexist man beat her. My wife, Bonnie (who has given her life to serve people marginalized by poverty, domestic violence, and mental illness), and Maggie (a high school senior considering studying political science and human rights in college) have been supportive readers, critics, and conversation partners as this project progressed. (Maggie has demanded co-author credit: I hope this mention appeases her.)

Another who has contributed to my thinking and writing about preaching in the era of Trump is the Reverend Ron Luckey. This second Ron in my life read every word, pushed me in directions I had not yet gone, and served as a companion on every step of this journey. He is one of the best preachers I have known, and his insights have added more to this project than I can name.

Finally, I need to thank Brad Lyons and Chalice Press for their willingness to publish this work at record speed. I am sure there will be many books to appear in the coming months and years that will deal with elements of Trump's election and presidency from various theological and critical perspectives and in a more in-depth manner than this work allows. This book is simply meant to be an initial volley into that court to help preachers deal with some of the strident rhetoric and policies that promise to cause chaos during Trump's time in office.

In the first half of the book, I offer some commentary on broad issues raised by Trump's campaign that will presumably continue to manifest themselves during his presidency. Specifically, the role of the pulpit in responding to our current situation must be informed by a range of perspectives. In the second half, I turn our attention to the issue of social justice related to specific groups Trump has targeted. Neither Donald Trump nor his supporters created the oppression these groups experience, but their bigoted and hate-filled rhetoric suggests deep problems and fears are likely to intensify in the coming days.

This book is not meant to be an exhaustive socio-political, theological, ethical, or even homiletical analysis of Trump's candidacy and presidency. It is intended to be a help to preachers who want to speak faithfully in response to the destructiveness of Trump's agenda and early days of the presidency.

O. Wesley Allen Jr.

Martin Luther King Jr. Day, January 16, 2017
(In the most prophetic of fashions, MLK day starts the week that will end with Trump's inauguration.)

PART I

BROAD ISSUES

As pastors consider whether and how to deal with Trump's oppressive rhetoric and proposed policies, there are background issues to consider. In the following essays that open this book, I offer my reflections on a variety of foundational issues for preachers to consider in light of the election of Donald Trump, and the potential for significant harm that his presidency could do to the ethical fabric of our society. While I at times turn to specific homiletical suggestions in these chapters, most of that sort of work is reserved for the second half of the book.

These reflections, then, are offered as contributions to the conversations many preachers are having internally as well as with clergy colleagues and lay members of the church. I would not expect readers to agree with every perspective I offer, but I hope that even in disagreeing with me, preachers find their views sharpened in a way that helps them better determine how to preach in this critical time.

CHAPTER 1

Confessing Our Shock and Awe

I'll admit it. When real estate mogul and reality show star Donald J. Trump came riding down the escalator at Trump Tower to announce his candidacy for the presidency in June 2015, I didn't take him seriously. I viewed him as a rich huckster turned reality star in a show I couldn't stand. I took the way he talked about himself as a sign of a needed-diagnosis of narcissistic megalomania. And I was aghast at the way he spoke about others, especially Mexican immigrants as rapists and drug dealers. As time progressed, I was confounded when he didn't immediately reject endorsements by David Duke and the KKK newspaper, *The Crusader*. But that is not what I need to confess. I need to confess my own hubris in assuming everyone else would see Trump in the same way I did. I need to confess the progressive bubble in which I lived that shielded me from even having to imagine that there were enough Americans with an ideology, and even a sense of proper public etiquette and civility, so far from my own that Trump stood even the smallest of chances of being elected.

So not taking him seriously, and assuming others would not (could not) either, I followed his candidacy with intrigue. As a Democrat, I have rarely watched Republican primary debates, but, during this election cycle, I couldn't take my eyes off the train wreck. I binge watched coverage of the debates and the campaign trail to see what Trump would say next. What names would he call the other Republican contenders? How would he attack journalists (even *Fox News* journalists!) for being "unfair" to him by asking hard questions? What outrageous claim would he make without any factual support? What segment of our populace would he offend next? How would he go off message this time and be unable to keep racist, misogynist, classist inferences from vomiting forth from his dark soul? I confess that I was entertained in my disgust and assumed that most others in this country, regardless of political orientation, viewed him as I did.

And then he started winning primaries. *It can't be so!* Then he won the Republican nomination. *Really? How?* And then...*no*...and then...*yes*...he won the general election. *The first president to follow the first African American president is going to be this man? The pendulum could not possibly swing that far back to the right!* And I finally turned off the television set late into the night of November 9, 2016. I couldn't bear to watch any more what before I couldn't stop myself from watching.

I now I find myself writing these words as President-elect Trump (yes, "President-elect"!) and his *Apprentice* version of a transition team work to fill out his cabinet. I write out of the fear, shock, and very real grief I feel, and which I think much of America feels. But the fact that he was elected means there are many people (at least 50 percent of the voting population, minus two or three million) who do not feel what I feel—or who are at least willing and able to overlook things I cannot. And that is what troubles me most. It was not that a person who holds and promotes views I find so abhorrent could run for office—after all, I hail from the state of George Wallace. But I could not fathom that the America I know and love, and that people in the

Church in which I profess faith when reciting the Creed and serve as clergyperson, could elect him.

My surprise likely reveals my social location. I am a white, Protestant, heterosexual, well-educated, middle-class male. I am the very image of American privilege. I have experienced the best benefits our culture has to offer. Even as a progressive who cares about social change, I have not personally felt the need for society to change so that the state of my well-being might improve. But many African Americans, women, immigrants, homosexuals, Muslims, and poor people are not surprised at all. They know how high the level of hatred and oppression in America (and in the Church) is—even if it has been expressed more subtly, while we had an African American president, than in the past and in the present. Many of them saw Trump expressing what they assume many people who look like me really think and feel. They were likely neither surprised by Trump's election nor by the way his election has emboldened and legitimized renewed hate speech against minorities in the wake of that election.

Saturday Night Live offered a particularly insightful commentary on this situation in a skit in which a group of friends gathered to watch the election results.[1] At 6:00 p.m., all of the white progressives in the apartment were ready to celebrate Hillary Clinton's election, but the lone Black friend (played by Dave Chappelle) interjects sarcastic remarks showing he expects Trump to win. As the evening progresses, hour by hour, the white friends move from joy to denial to despondency. Finally, at midnight, after all of the swing states have swung toward Trump, one of the white friends has a revelation: "Oh, my God, I think America is racist." Dave Chappelle's character responds sarcastically and hyperbolically while the recently entered Chris Rock feigns a look of surprise, "Oh, my God! You know, I remember my great-grandfather told me something like that. [Then dismissively] But he was like a slave or something. I don't know."

As someone whose life and livelihood will likely change little due to the election of a candidate like Trump, I have no right, or desire, to represent the voices, experiences, or concerns of those truly threatened by a Trump presidency. I pray that what I write, instead, is an expression of solidarity with those who are very much at risk if Trump institutes many of the proposals he made during his campaign (which at the moment seems to be the case, given the kinds of cabinet and agency appointments he is lining up). I write as a progressive Christian of European descent who feels fear, anger, grief, and especially shame following the election of a leader who manifested such a lack of decorum and promoted such hatred. My fear, anger, and grief are rooted in the fact that America is so divided at the moment along lines of race, gender, class, religion, and sexual orientation. My shame is rooted in the fact that we—yes, *we*; not *they*; we, the American populace, and we, the American church—voted out of fear and hatred to promote these divisions further. I am ashamed that white, patriarchal America voted to restore a status quo of bygone years in an attempt to protect "us" from "them."

Specifically, I write to reflect on the role of the pulpit at the beginning of this new era of Trump's presidency. I write to and for preachers who feel called to speak prophetically over against the kinds of mean-spirited rhetoric and potentially oppressive policies we have seen in the election and expect during his time in office. I write not only to address how to preach "about" issues raised by Trump, but how to preach to a divided America that exists in and around a divided church. I write as someone striving to figure out how the church in the U.S. is to participate faithfully in the *missio Dei* (the mission of God) in the American era of Trump's presidency.

It is important to acknowledge that I write at a different time than you read. I am writing prior to Trump's inauguration. My "data" comes from Trump's election rhetoric and promises and the early days of his post-election transition. I pray that this book is unnecessary and Trump's presidency looks and sounds radically different than did his campaign. I would love for the office to remake the man instead of the man remaking the office. But signs at the moment of my writing do not make me hopeful. I have no faith that the power that comes with his new office will temper his approach or attitude.

CHAPTER 2

A Postmodern Presidency

Much of my scholarly work has focused on proposals for how to preach during postmodernity.[1] In my estimation, postmodernism has reached a new stage of development in American society with the election of Donald Trump—one I have not addressed in these earlier works. And this new stage of development has much to say about how we proclaim God's good news in our sermons.

Postmodernism

The word *postmodern* signals that its definition is related to the definition of *modern*. What comes after modernity? It is helpful to back up a little further, actually, to premodernism and then work through modernism, to get a full view of what is unique about postmodernism.

In a premodern worldview, truth is seen as absolute and universal. Something cannot, by definition, be true here and false there, true now and false then. What is true in Rome is true in Jerusalem and Alexandria and Beijing and on Mars. What was true in 568 BCE was also true in 1024 CE, is true now, and will be true until the end of time. In this worldview, revelation is the primary authority and source of truth. God (or gods) declare what is true; and if our reason conflicts with such revelation, our reason must be flawed. Since the Bible says that God created the world in six days, science must be wrong in promoting the big bang and evolution as natural processes that took millions of years to form the universe in its present state.

A modern worldview also sees truth as absolute and universal. The primary source and authority for truth, however, has shifted to reason. With the rise of the scientific method and the philosophical search for a foundation of knowledge during the Enlightenment, the human mind was elevated over religion in determining truth—reason over revelation. Modernists viewed religious claims that contradicted science as, at worst, superstitious mythology or, at best, theological claims of a different order than scientific ones. Since science has shown that it took millions of years of natural processes for the universe to evolve to its present state, the story of God creating the world in six days must be interpreted as nonliteral if truth is to be found in it at all.

This brings us to postmodernism. In a postmodern worldview, truth is viewed as local or relative. "That may be true for you, but not for me." In other words, "truth" itself has been redefined. Or, I would argue, what has happened is that a concern for *meaning* has supplanted the premodern and modern concern for truth (even though people still use the word *truth* to name what they mean as "meaningful." As evangelical theologian Stanley J. Grenz argues, the concern of postmoderns is not whether some claim is true so much as a concern for what it does, what results from the claim.[2] Instead of *discovering* truth external to myself (be it in revelation or reason), I *construct* meaning of the world external to me in ways that are useful to me. Indeed, I am suspicious of hierarchical claims of authority that pronounce what I should hold as true. Thus, postmoderns hold experience to be the primary authority for making meaning over against revelation or reason. This allows postmoderns to draw on multiple sources for making meaning—a dash of biology, a pinch of Christianity, a spoonful of Eastern philosophy, all mixed together with a cup full of political ideology shaped by parents and teachers and colleagues. Or, they can choose a central source for making meaning—say, Christianity—while being completely comfortable with others choosing different sources to make meaning for themselves. Postmoderns can decide at any moment whether a creation story or scientific explanation of the origins of the universe and life are more experientially meaningful.

If this is postmodernism, I consider myself a light postmodernist. The rejection of a hegemony of hierarchical truth-claims asserted by those who most benefit from the status quo that those claims support is potentially liberating for many on this planet. Postmodernism wrenches power to determine what is true or meaningful from a few at the top of society and distributes this power widely. Put differently, the construction of meaning is democratized in postmodernity in a way I highly value.

On the other hand, the very fact that I as a Christian and a preacher find ancient scripture as valuable for understanding and addressing contemporary human experience(s) means that I see some expressions of meaning as having import beyond local social contexts.[3] I may have no interest in arguing for my worldview as being absolutely and universally true, but I do find it to be of ultimate value for me.

Thus, I have argued for a light postmodern homiletical approach that is conversational in nature. Instead of pronouncing truth from on high, sermons should serve as a resource for congregations as they make meaning in conversation with many different sources of meaning in their lives and world.

Postmodern Campaign

But the other shoe of postmodernism dropped with the election of Donald Trump—a shoe that worries me. Throughout the election, Trump had little concern for facts—

that is, for what has counted as truth in past elections. He was quite willing to say that he had "heard" something from someone he respects or that he read something "online," and then speak about the subject in the same way candidates and politicians would only speak about confirmed facts in the past. He was willing to make accusations (such as vote tampering) without any evidence. He was comfortable with broad generalizations concerning groups of people or issues that lacked any nuance. He was willing to counter what authorities said (such as security agencies claiming Russia was behind the hacking of the Democratic campaign's emails) if he didn't like their claims. He was willing to cite tabloids (especially one published by a friend of his) as the basis for charges against other candidates (such as Ted Cruz's father participating in John F. Kennedy's assassination). He was even willing to assert that he never made such-and-such a claim and thus his current claim was not a contradiction to an earlier position even though a journalist would quote his previous comments in detail. It is no wonder Trump was so reluctant to apologize for things he said, even to the point of justifying comments about grabbing women's genitals as "locker room" talk. If there is no possibility of him being wrong in factual terms, then his opinion can't be wrong either.

What is perhaps more striking is that so many of Trump's supporters simply didn't care that he didn't care about facts. While those of us supporting other candidates again and again would yell at our television sets every time he said what we thought contradicted clear facts, his supporters never wavered. He was perhaps correct when he claimed that he could shoot someone on Fifth Avenue in New York City and not lose any voters. He was correct because his voters did not care about the truth or falseness of what he said. They cared about how his rhetoric spoke to their experience, how it expressed their own experience of anger and fear. In other words, Trump's supporters found things he said to be meaningful to them regardless of whether they were true or not.

This situation was generally acknowledged by the editors of the *Oxford English Dictionary* when one week after the presidential election, they chose "post-truth" as their word for the year in 2016. The definition they provide is, "Relating to or denoting circumstances in which objective facts are less influential in shaping public opinion than appeals to emotion and personal belief."[4] They might as well have chosen Stephen Colbert's 2005-coined term, "truthiness," highlighting the difference between thinking about something and knowing it in your gut regardless of any logic or facts.[5]

Moreover, during this election cycle, social media was swamped with fake news—lies purported to be truth as opposed to even "truthiness," which is at least sincerely believed. While not limited to election issues, a preponderance of fake news stories were written to make wild allegations about candidates opposing Donald Trump and/or public personalities that were perceived to have challenged Trump during the campaign, and many such stories were promoted by Trump's campaign. One such example was #Pizzagate, in which it was claimed that a Washington, D.C., pizzeria (that had corresponded with the Clinton campaign concerning a fundraising dinner) was a site for a child sex trafficking operation that involved Clinton campaign staff. General Michael Flynn (the president-elect's national security advisor!) had posted on Twitter a week before the election that Clinton and her staff were involved in pedophilia, money laundering, and other crimes. Then his son, who was also his father's chief of staff and an advisor to Trump, pushed the conspiracy theory concerning the pizzeria. All of this led to an armed man entering the pizzeria and firing a weapon in order to try to rescue children. He surrendered to police upon finding no evidence of a sex trade operation, but Flynn Jr. continued to argue the case might be valid.

While the case resulted in the Flynn Jr.'s dismissal from the Trump transition team, much damage was already done and many still choose to believe the child slavery case to be open. Indeed, the shooter himself, after being arrested, refused to dismiss the "truth" of the stories about a Clinton-sponsored sex slave trade, admitting only that there were no children at the particular location he investigated.

In 2006, *Time* chose "You" as its Person of the Year. The choice was meant to celebrate that the many who created content on the web had wrenched power from the few who usually created content for public consumption. In 2016, *Time,* of course, selected Donald Trump for the recognition. There is a sense in which Trump receiving the award could not have happened without the content revolution acknowledged a decade earlier.

While there are many positive elements to the democratizing of consumable content, one downside is that content can be posted regardless of any standards of factuality, truth, or the like. There is no regulating body, such as an editorial team of a newspaper, to refuse publication of content because it lacks credibility. And, in a postmodern age, consumers will pick and choose what to consume based on their previously held ideologies and experiences. They will lift up some claims made by "you" and reject others based on outcomes they find useful. They may *say* they believe what some post, video, or article asserts based on it being "true," but the standard of truth from a modern worldview has little bearing on such postmodern belief.

It is important to note I am not talking about policy views in the current state of believing in something without being concerned about facts. I am not talking about Democrats versus Republicans. Democracy, especially a two-party system such as America's, is rooted in debate about best policy. In other words, disagreement about best routes forward on different issues is key to the way our government functions. Conservatives, moderates, and liberals argue for their views, and then a majority decides policy. Postmodernism is not a conservative or progressive issue. Postmoderns are not of one mind concerning big versus small government, how we should deal with the violence in the Middle East, or whether the Affordable Care Act should be upheld or repealed. Postmodernism does, however, shape the way people make meaning in relation to these issues and how they interpret the rhetoric that's used to discuss the issues.

The "anything goes" approach to reality is the negative, even dangerous, side of postmodernism. If I *want* something to be meaningful, it is. If I want Trump to be right, he is. It doesn't matter what others say. It doesn't matter how the facts look. It doesn't matter what harm a claim I find meaningful might have on others. Such an approach to making meaning can be difficult to counter from the pulpit.

The Postmodern Pulpit

Liberal theology was at the heart of Mainline Protestant theology that embraced the modernist worldview in the nineteenth and much of the twentieth centuries. Of course, the "liberal" in "liberal theology" doesn't mean the same thing as when we use it in the current political scene as a synonym for "progressive." Liberal theology, like "liberal arts" education, strove to liberate people from superstitious ways of thinking, believing, and acting inherited from the past. Traditional theology had to be updated, revised, or reinterpreted to be sensible for people who embrace a scientific worldview.

Accompanying modernity's confidence in the human mind was a confidence in human ability to do the right thing (individually) and to make the world a just place (corporately). Thus in relation to social issues, liberal theology assumed that if injustices and suffering in the world were shown to people with means, and a reasonable way to address the causes of injustice and suffering were provided, people would and could act to eradicate them. In other words, liberal theologians believed educating people would lead to the best society possible—indeed, to the arrival of God's reign. This way of thinking basically died and was buried in the 1940s. The very technologies that human reason was able to invent and that liberal theology thought could be used to cure the ills of the world were turned back on the world in a process of exterminating nearly twelve million people (six million of whom were Jews) during the Holocaust and drawing nearly the entire planet into World War II.

Though liberal theology's confidence in human ability and desire to do what is right and just may have been lost, the basic approach to preaching that grew out of liberal theology is still very much alive. When dealing with social issues, preachers still try to educate their congregations into doing peace and justice work in the world. They still think (hope?) quoting statistics about hunger will make people give up their TVs and cars to eradicate poverty. They strive to use logic to persuade people about what they should do.

Certainly this type of education in the pulpit is still needed—information does inform, after all. So I am not advocating that we throw all facts out of our sermons. But modernist argumentation cannot be the *primary* homiletical approach employed. There are two problems with this liberal homiletical approach in relation to preaching during the postmodern presidency.

First, while the liberal approach informs, it does not challenge, inspire, motivate, or invite hearers to examine their self-interest, *vis-à-vis* a particular social ill. Knowledge is simply unable to put a chink in the armor of sin. Paul is correct when he says, "I do not understand my own actions. For I do not do what I want, but I do the very thing I hate" (Rom. 7:15). We are trapped in sin and cannot by our own means escape it. Our imprisonment is all the more evident when we consider our participation in structural sin—that is, in societal systems that oppress and cause suffering. If I directly harm someone with my words, I am more aware of my guilt than when I purchase clothes made in a sweatshop in Bangladesh. And while I may be able to curtail my tongue so I do less harm to others with my speech, I am unable (or at least feel unable) to dismantle the economic systems by which First World consumers thrive on the backs of Third World workers. All of this is to say that *informing* congregations about the damage of Trump's Alt-right rhetoric and the threat of oppressive federal policies will do little to get our hearers to work for a different vision for the world in the name of Christ.

Second, liberal approaches to preaching were not concerned with experience. Modernism valued intellect over emotion. Information and facts are simply not the way to get to the postmodern's heart. If we didn't see that before, the election results should be like getting a new prescription for our eyeglasses. Information is a way to persuade modernists who care about truth. Preachers in a postmodern context, however, must find ways to offer to their congregations *experiences* of those events, stories, values, and ideas from which they hope the hearers will make meaning.

Moreover, one-time experiences will not have much of an effect in a postmodern context. People make meaning in a cafeteria fashion, picking and choosing amongst a range of options, experimenting with this or that dish. A sermon is one little item on the salad bar in the postmodern cafeteria, squeezed in between the shredded cheese and the banana pudding. We speak for fifteen to thirty minutes on a Sunday, but our hearers are listening to other voices every hour, every day, all week long. The postmodern population is a plugged-in population. People have their televisions, radios, computers, and smart phones going all the time—often simultaneously. They get information and proposals for making meaning constantly. One sermon will rarely change a congregation's mindset about anything in this climate, much less be able to compete with Trump's seemingly non-stop tweeting.

So in the era of Trump, pastors must plan on addressing topics of concern raised by his campaign and time in office repeatedly from the pulpit. The true power of the pulpit is less in the individual sermon and more in the cumulative effect of preaching to the same congregation week in and week out over the course of years. We must offer our hearers multiple experiences of an issue over time if we hope for it to take hold in them. One scoop of gospel perspective on any topic from the salad bar will hardly nourish the congregation for long.

Likewise, it's important to remember that it is not the preacher's job simply to preach the gospel; it is the preacher's job to get the gospel heard, then believed, and then lived. This not only takes time and repetition. It takes approaching difficult subjects in a hospitable manner—inviting hearers into the sermons as honored guests to converse about the topic instead of using the topic as a weapon against them (or against Trump) in the fashion of a take-it-or-leave-it debate. In the coming chapters we will explore different strategies for achieving this posture during the sermon in relation to different topics. For now, suffice it to say that we must be careful in our attempts to counter the rhetoric and attitudes of President Trump—that we, *in no way,* emulate his tone and rhetoric. We preach a gospel of justice, mercy, grace, and hope; and our sermons, whatever the topic, should be appropriate to that gospel.

CHAPTER 3

The Elephant in the Church

The first step in addressing a problem is to admit that there is one. We pastors repeat this trope to people who come to us for counseling all the time. When this problem concerns a group embroiled in conflict, such as a family, we might say, "It is important to name the elephant in the room in order to deal with the elephant in the room."

Well, there is an elephant in the church. And it is important that we name it. First, though, we must be clear what elephant we are not naming. While the title of the chapter is intended as a pun related to the Republican party's mascot, progressive pastors and congregations know (and value) that the Republican elephant is in their congregation, just as conservative congregations are aware (and value) that the Democrats' donkey is in theirs. Liberal and conservative politics do not always align with liberal and conservative theologies. The body of Christ has many parts and is expansive enough to be strengthened by diverse political ideologies in its midst. Ecclesiological and ecclesiastical unity need not be defined by uniformity. After all, Paul called on the Philippians to be of one mind, to have the self-emptying mind of Christ as they dealt with one another in a time of conflict (Phil. 2:1–11). He didn't instruct the Philippians to all think alike. So as we preachers think about addressing issues that will arise in the Trump era, we must be clear that the elephant in the church that needs to be named is not the Republican elephant.

This elephant in the church, at least in the white church, is the Republican elephant trained through abuse by Trump to do any trick for applause and a peanut. Part of the training, however, includes the fact that at any moment this elephant could go on a rampage through the circus tent—just as it did during the campaign, and following, in terms of hate speech and actions. It is not only a three-ton animal we all tiptoe around; it is a powerful animal that can start stomping around, pushing pews out of its way like sticks on a path, picking up the cross with its trunk and casting it aside, and breaking the altar/table into pieces with its mighty tusks. It can mock people with disabilities because those of us without are tired of making accommodations. It can call gay people in and out of the church "faggots" without any shame at all. It can wear a hat that says "Make America Great Again" which really means "Make America White Again." It is time we name this elephant as the really @REALdonaldtrump and make clear it has no place in the church.

In other words, we pastors have no problem with the fact that our churches are filled with both Republicans and Democrats. We who find Trump to be a threat to much of what we value can have no problem with the fact that some people in our church voted for him in order to support the Republican party platform (in spite of him), or as a vote against other candidates such as Hillary Clinton. We can rationalize someone voting for Trump reluctantly. Our problem in the church, the truly worrisome elephant in the church that we are afraid to name, is that we likely have members of our congregation who voted for Trump specifically *because* they share some of his unacceptable views we find contrary to the good news of Jesus Christ. There are people to whom we preach who share Trump's xenophobic (especially Islamophobic), sexist, racist, heterosexist, classist, ableist, nationalist idolatry of self and tribe. This elephant refuses to dance when the children's choir sings,

> Jesus loves the little children, all the children of the world
> Red and yellow, black and white; they are precious in
> his sight.

This elephant trumpets loudly over the lector when she reads the words of Jesus, "My house shall be called a house of prayer for all the nations" (Mk. 11:17). It sprays water all over the sanctuary to distract from a baptism that includes Paul's baptismal formula:

> There is no longer Jew or Greek, there is no longer
> slave or free, there is no longer male and female; for
> all of you are one in Christ Jesus. (Gal. 3:28)

The problem of this elephant in the church is complicated by the fact that we preachers love (many of) the people who brought the elephant in. They are part of our flock, our church family. And yet we may also be scared of (many of) them in the sense that we fear if we preach on issues like those named above which offend us greatly, these people will turn on us. So we face a double temptation.

We are tempted, on the one hand, to avoid these issues in the pulpit, to avoid dealing with the elephant in the nave (and the chancel?) and hope it will continue residing in our midst without doing too much damage. We are tempted to preach spirituality, self-help messages, and a gospel of individual grace. We are tempted to soothe our consciences by saying the pulpit is not a bully pulpit, and proclamation and politics have nothing to do with one another.

We are tempted, on the other hand, to shout out, "Damn, the torpedoes!" and forge ahead to preach on the above topics as one doing battle with Trump and his supporters. We are tempted not just to name and address the elephant in the church but to attack it like a wild boar in *Lord of the*

Flies. We are tempted to take names, point fingers, and ask, "How could you!?" We are tempted to don the mantle of the angry prophet, speaking truth to power regardless of the consequences.

Preachers, however, are called to care very much about the consequences of our sermons. Granted, we should care a little less than we do about people *liking* us for our sermons. But we don't simply serve the content of the theological and ethical claims of Christian traditions; we also serve the church to whom this content is given. When we step into the pulpit, our job is not simply to proclaim the gospel but to get the gospel heard—to get it heard so that it might be believed and lived. Neither ignoring the elephant in the sanctuary nor verbally berating it will accomplish this.

The Pulse of the Congregation

If we are going to get a new interpretation of the gospel heard, believed, and lived that challenges the status quo defended by Trump and his strongest supporters, we must have a sound understanding of the current division in the nation and the church. Such understanding does not require a degree in political science or sociology, so much as a serious evaluation of what we already know. Any map of blue and red states shows that the country's coasts have a majority of Democrats and the Bible and Rust Belts in the middle of the country have a majority of Republicans. We could likely map the pews in our congregations in similar ways.

The division in the country, however, is of a different character than simple differences in political ideologies. What actually unites those on both sides of the divide is anger and fear. White, patriarchal America elected Donald Trump to the office of president out of a sense of anxiety and disenfranchisement in relation to a loss of status and privilege they have experienced with the growing pluralism and globalism in the late twentieth and early twenty-first centuries. Millennials supported Bernie Sanders in relation to anxiety and disenfranchisement they feel in relation to their future looking bleaker than the futures of earlier generations due to the massive wealth of the 1 percent in relation to the other 99 percent. People of color and women who supported Hillary Clinton experience anxiety and disenfranchisement in relation to Donald Trump's campaign rhetoric that essentially relegates them to second-class citizens or noncitizens to be deported. There are intense emotions on all sides of the political chasm that look very similar even though they are rooted in very different causes. One of the reasons these emotions are so difficult to address in a diverse community such as a congregation is that much of the anger and fear is directed at those who hold different political views and different positions in society—that is, those sitting "across the aisle" in the nave.

In this situation, people in the pews experience the same kinds of temptations as the preacher. On the one hand, they are tempted to think the best way to deal with this division and its related emotions is to ignore them. Congregations often prefer civility to honesty. We can all get along with each other and the elephant in the room if the preacher will just mind his or her own business. On the other hand, there is the temptation to hope the preacher will preach about social justice issues related to the recent campaign and the future Trump presidency that will support their worldview and condemn the sins of the other camps. Preachers must be careful not to give in to either temptation of their members.

Cleaning the Elephant Dung Out of the Church

Preachers are called to be prophets who address, indeed counter, the kinds of oppressive intentions Trump has expressed during his campaign. We cannot claim to serve a God of justice and be silent about such things in the pulpit. On the other hand, we're also called to be pastors to *all* of the members of our flock—to care for *all* the souls in our congregation, not just those with whom we agree. We cannot claim to serve the God of mercy and fail to offer grace to those who disagree with us about issues raised by a Trump presidency.

The order should almost always be a movement from pastor to prophet instead of the other way around. If we sound off as a prophet without our congregation (or members of it) knowing and trusting that we care for them, they will never accept us as *either* pastor or prophet. If, instead, we first establish a strong pastoral relationship with our congregation (and *all* of its members), then they will trust us when we claim a prophetic voice, whether they agree with our stance or not.

One of my pastoral heroes is Dan Whitsett. He served the church in Alabama in which I grew up years before I was born, but his legend hung around long after he was gone. He was called to the church in the late Forties or early Fifties.

Dan was a visiting pastor in the sense that he visited people in their homes so much no one was sure if he ever lived in the parsonage. He listened to youth instead of just preaching at them. In that church, he baptized babies, confirmed the youth, married the young adults, and buried the dead. He was especially known for the love he showed when people were sick. If someone was in the hospital, he got there before the doctor. He loved those people and they loved him.

While Dan was serving that church, the decision in Brown v. The Board of Education was announced in 1954. Of course, it would be nearly ten years before that decision was implemented in Alabama. But Dan Whitsett began right away preaching that Christians should support integration of the schools, and that in fact they should view all of God's children as equal. He used what he learned in seminary; he used his spiritual gifts in scripture, theology, ethics, sociology, and psychology to argue for this justice issue. So in the mid-Fifties, when most white pulpits in Alabama heard a domesticated distortion of the gospel, First Methodist

Church in Sylacauga, Alabama, heard God calling them into the reign of God in a radically new way. They heard a call to overcome the divisions in society between whites and Blacks.

The Ku Klux Klan began riding around the outside of the church honking their horns during the worship hour. Swastikas were painted on the church doors more than once. And a cross was burned in the front yard of the parsonage.

Some church members left, but most people stayed and supported Rev. Whitsett. I suspect that, to some degree, many sat in the pews with their arms folded and cotton balls in their ears, but they stayed. They stayed and tolerated Dan because he was their pastor before he was their prophet. Others, though, were moved from their racism of the past to a pro-integration position rooted in the gospel they heard from Rev. Whitsett, which they were now trying to live.

Being pastoral prophets means we must, in our sermons, not only give our hearers room to grow in the direction we hope, but also room to disagree with us, even when we think such disagreement is rooted in selfishness, bigotry, or hatred. In a postmodern world, if we preach a progressive ethic with the sense that "God said, I believe it, and that settles it for me," hearers we most want to convert will reject anything we have to say.

Our sermons need to invite conversation about difficult topics instead of trying to put the punctuation on the end of those conversations. We need to open up congregational space for honest conversation in the place of divisive debate in which someone wins and someone loses. Conversation, as a postmodern form of communication, values diversity and reciprocity without saying, "Anything goes." A pastor who desires to hear what a congregant who disagrees with him has to say in order to appreciate the person and where she is coming from will be able to speak to and be heard by that person in ways a nonpastoral prophet never will.

CHAPTER 4

Us and Them

After the election, I talked to a friend from Allentown, Pennsylvania, on the phone. I began the call by jokingly blaming him for Donald Trump's election. "Why am I to blame?" he asked. I explained that I voted in Texas—no one ever really expected Texas to do anything but support the Republican candidate. "Texas is *red*—from the barbeque sauce slathered on brisket to almost every elected office for which it votes," I pointed out. "But Pennsylvania is a swing state! You didn't do your job!"

We laughed...sort of. And then, speaking from the middle of that swing state, he said to me, "I have always believed there is a deep, core human need for love and grace. This election taught me that there is also a deep human need for hate." He explained how humanity usually keeps such hatred in check with religious codes, societal norms, parenting guidance, laws, and the like. But as soon as we see a legitimizing force forming that serves as a tipping point, we latch onto the opportunity to exercise that need for hate again. As he saw it, Trump's campaign and election served as that legitimizing force, allowing white America to bring to the surface their essential, yet despicable (yes, deplorable) need to hate and express it in the forms of racism, misogyny, homophobia, and classism.

I have thought about this lesson a lot since he said it—especially since there has been a significant rise in hate speech and hate crimes since Trump was elected. Within *just ten days after the election,* the Southern Poverty Law Center had collected reports of 867 incidents of harassment and intimidation![1] Just a few examples:

- In San Diego, a driver yelled at a person crossing the street, "F*****g n****r, go back to Africa! The slave ship is loading up! TRUMP!"

- In Colorado Springs, eighth-grade students told Latino students on the school bus, "Not only should Trump build a wall, but it should be electrocuted [*sic*] and Mexicans should have to wear shock collars."

- In Arlington, Virginia, a woman crossing the street reported that two young white men yelled at her from their car: "You better be ready, because with Trump, we can grab you by the p***y even if you don't want it."

- At a hospital in Chicago, a woman reported that a man in the elevator looked at her and said, "F***n' sand-n****r. Thank God Trump is now president. He's gonna deport your terrorist ass."

- In Denver, a transgender woman's car was spray-painted with a swastika and the words "Trump" and "die," among other derogatory terms.

These incidents seem to indicate that my friend is onto something. It looks like we humans need to hate...or at least that we really *want* to. By the time you read this book, the number of incidents of harassment will likely have increased exponentially, and you may completely agree with my friend.

Communal Identity

At the point at which I am writing, however, I want to hold to a belief that humans do not have a *need* for hate. Instead, I think (I hope!) the hatred we are seeing (and have experienced in myriad horrific ways throughout human history) is a perversion of a different core human need and characteristic.

For all the ways individualism has been elevated and celebrated in modern and postmodern Western society, human identity is rooted in communal identity. Humans are pack animals. The earliest humans survived as gatherers and hunters by banding together against wild beasts and the forces of nature. This dynamic naturally evolved into "drawing lines in the sand"—by which a group of humans claimed certain land as "ours"—and was accompanied by a willingness to defend against others who would try to take the land. The best and worst of tribalism, nationalism, ethnic and religious devotion, and the like grew across the millennia of human history.

In light of this claim, we can see that the modernist idea of the United States as a "melting pot" was not only a myth, it was misguided. Humans have a basic need to categorize the world in terms of "us" and "them," and when we try to force everyone into a lowest-common-denominator kind of "us," the pot is bound to boil over. There will be dissatisfaction from the majority in power that others have not assimilated gratefully, and distress by minorities lacking power to avoid their unique identity being devalued and erased.

The church has contributed to this state of affairs. On the one hand, the modern, Enlightenment church sought to evangelize the whole world in the sense of spreading the "one truth" to all people. To a great extent, however, this mission was an attempt to colonize the world so that all looked, sounded, thought, and acted like "us" in the West. On the other hand, much of the evolving postmodern church has sought to embrace a "think and let think" ethic to its standards of membership, so that anyone can join the church and participate in its life with few barriers of theology, ethics, or morals getting in the way. In this stance, the church is trying to live out God's inclusive love by being a fully inclusive community. We can, however, profess belief in both a God who offers unconditional grace and the "one, holy, catholic, and apostolic" church while still recognizing the *need* for healthy boundaries to our community of faith and identity.

A Lesson from Structuralism

Structuralism is a hermeneutical, sociological, philosophical approach that assumes human culture and communication are best understood by uncovering structures underlying the way humans think, act, and feel. A key element of this methodology is the assumption that these underlying structures mean every thought, action, or feeling stands in relationship with other thoughts, actions, and feelings. One of the basic such relationships is that of contrast. Any word, for instance, has meaning by virtue of contrast with another word. Take the word *woman*. We may think that this word has a definition prescribed by Webster's dictionary that tells us what it means. Contrast, however, tells us the force of a word in different contexts. If I describe a person as a "woman" in contrast to a "man," I am saying something about her sex or gender. If, however, I describe a person as a "woman" in contrast to a "girl," I am saying something about her age or maturity.

When we recognize, then, that words and concepts have meaning in terms of contrasts, we must recognize the same is true of identities. "Us," only and always, is defined over against "them." There is no "us" without a "them." The contrasting approach to humans defining ourselves in communal terms is, I believe, a core human instinct and need. When we as a society (or as a church) deny or ignore this need, unhealthy expressions of communal identities arise. And this situation, I think, is what in part led to the election of a candidate who spouted devaluing and hateful speech about a range of "thems." "We" feel better about us when "they" are placed on a lower step than us on the staircase of society. Donald Trump tapped into the low self-esteem of much of white America and promised them a higher value by degrading a range of "others."

Preaching a Healthier Us and Them

If the church (and society) has been mistaken in both its attempts to missionize/colonize the world to bring all into "us" and to reduce any sense of a "them" with a *laissez-faire* approach to inclusion in the community, what is a better, healthier approach to the human need to divide the world into us and them?

First, preachers must work to rid the church (and society) of the sin of viewing the contrast between "us" and "them" in hierarchical terms. Difference can mean "distinction from" without always implying better or worse. A woman is different from a man or a girl, but her difference implies neither that she is better or worse than the other two.

The first church I served, as a part-time student pastor while in college in the mid-1980s, was in a tiny town in Alabama (the population at the time was in the 600s) that had once been a coal mine camp. When the coal mine closed down, the only white people who stayed were those who couldn't afford to leave, or had nowhere to go. At that point, poorer African American families began moving in, because they could afford the small four-room houses that had been built by the mining company for white miners and their families in the early twentieth century.

The town was so small that none of the churches had numbers or resources to have any significant ministry with children. In the spring, I proposed to my church board to sponsor a once-a-week, mid-week program where we brought together children and youth from all the churches. The mostly elderly congregation (with a worship attendance around 20) was thrilled to have an energetic young pastor (also 20), and the board voted unanimously to support the new ministry. I immediately began talking with other pastors in the town, publicizing the ministry, inviting children to come to Terrific Tuesdays, and recruiting volunteers from all the churches.

Just before the program was to begin the week after public school was out for the summer, the board chair called a meeting. They were aghast that I had invited the Black churches in the area to participate in the program. I was completely caught off guard that this was an issue in the church in 1985! I reminded them that I had said I would invite *all* the churches to participate, but they explained that they thought I would have known better than to include Blacks in my "all." After much debate, the board said they would approve the program only if I limited participation in the program to white children and volunteers. I refused, thinking surely they would be too ashamed actually to vote on such a blatantly racist motion and have their names recorded in the minutes. I was wrong. The vote was split, but there was a clear majority. The program was never launched.

I decided to resign from the church over the matter. How could these people call themselves the "body of Christ" and act in a manner so contrary to the gospel? But the chairperson of the personnel committee asked me to stay. She was one of the few who voted in favor of the program, and said I needed to stay and preach about racism instead of leaving the church to be unchallenged on the issue.

So I stayed. And I brought up issues of racism in the pulpit regularly. My sermons were blunt instruments as I tried to shame the congregation into being a better church. I argued repeatedly that in God's eyes there is no "us" and "them," so we should not hold such a view either.

I was young, naïve, and lacked sophistication in my theology and in my understanding of complex issues such as racism. Only years later—with distance, education, and experience—did I come to realize that the people in that congregation could only see themselves as near the bottom of society. They felt abandoned by the company to which they had given their lives. They saw little hope for a future any better than the present. The only thing that kept them from seeing themselves as being at the very bottom of society was the ability to view the African Americans in the town as lower than they were.

I do not mean to excuse their racism by naming their action in this way, or to erase the complexities of centuries of oppressive racism that contributed to their views. I simply mean to name that, in the immediate circumstances of the moment in which I was serving as their pastor, I should have addressed their racism differently in my sermons. I needed to begin by helping them see that differences between us and them do not imply a ranking of value. I needed to begin by naming that the contrast between their socio-economic situation and the wider world did not mean they were less than others in society. If I worked to raise their self-esteem in relation to the crushing contrast they experienced, then, perhaps I could have made movement with them in raising the esteem they accorded to the African Americans they considered to be "less than" they.

In addition to striving to rid the church (and society) of the sin of viewing the contrast between "us" and "them" in hierarchical terms, a second thing preachers can do to help the church (and society) embrace a healthier approach to the human need to divide the world into us and them is to foster the postmodern virtue of valuing a cafeteria-style approach to making meaning in relation to the differences between us and them. In a postmodern approach to the world, we make meaning through experiences of wildly diverse resources. We need not agree with them to learn from them, nor do we feel the need to try to convince all to agree with us. While something may be true/meaningful for you, that does not mean it has to be true/meaningful for me.

If we can apply this attitude to others—the "they" who identify differently than "we"—then we can appreciate and learn from people and groups wildly diverse from us as well. We can celebrate the differences instead of feeling the need either to reduce us all to sameness or label differences as "better" or "worse."

There was a congregation in Kentucky that began to experience growth due to members of the LGBTQ community beginning to attend. Long-timers at the church who viewed homosexuality as immoral and sinful tolerated the inclusion of gay men and lesbians as long as they put money in the offering plate, weren't too blatant in their sexuality, were a small minority in the congregation, and didn't assume leadership roles. But of course, as the number of gay attendees and members grew, tensions surfaced in the church.

The pastor scheduled a number of meetings for people to discuss the issue. But the same thing always happened: people on both sides of the issue starting throwing around Bible verses, and debate gave way to shouting matches. Then, on one occasion, the pastor started the meeting differently. He placed a loaf of bread and a chalice in the middle of the group. "After the meeting," he said, "we are going to share the Lord's Supper. You are going to pass the bread and wine to one another as a testimony to the fact that Christ died for everyone here, whether you agree with or like each other or not. So in the conversation, conduct yourselves in accordance with your understanding of the meal and the recognition that the elements are in our midst."

The conversation was different that night. Indeed, it was a conversation and not a debate. A gay man sincerely asked an older, straight man why he was so adamant that homosexuality was a sin. The older man named a fear he had about the truth of scripture: he worried about a slippery slope that if we didn't believe the scriptural verses condemning homosexuality, then we could just quit believing others as well. It would become a matter of what we like instead of what God calls us to believe, do, and be. Then the older man asked the younger, gay man, why he wanted to be in the church and believe in a Bible that condemns who he is. The younger man told his story of being raised in the church and how deeply he believed God loved him and that he knew this because of the ministry, death, and resurrection of Jesus Christ. He implied he couldn't help being a Christian any more than he could help being gay.

I have no idea if, at the end of the conversation, the men agreed with each other on anything. But they gained a new appreciation of each other and understood their differences better. And they were able to share and celebrate the body and blood of Christ with one another.

CHAPTER 5

Love Trumps Hate, But Only If We Love Trump

Whatever else Donald Trump did during the primaries and the general election, he elicited powerful emotions. He held large rallies in which crowds chanted loudly both for him and against his opponents. Violence erupted more than once—sometimes accompanied by Trump's directions to remove protestors or promises to pay for the defense costs for such violent acts. Many outside of the circle of Trump's camp of supporters saw these emotions as hatred inspired by the hate speech of the candidate.

Thus, one of the slogans that became popular at Hillary Clinton rallies was "Love Trumps Hate." For the Democrat's campaign, this slogan worked well to highlight the contrast between Trump's desire to build a wall, deport illegal immigrants, register Muslims, enforce "law and order" over addressing the killing of young, African American men and women by police, and judge the value of women based on their looks on the one hand, and Clinton's "big tent" approach to inclusion of the other. Indeed, while Trump's campaign focused on re-establishing the privileged status quo for white America, Clinton spoke of an America where power and resources were shared in many directions.

But if we are honest, those of us among the Clinton supporters can't claim to extend the love that trumps hate to Trump and his supporters themselves. Some of us voting against Trump have exhibited visceral emotions with intensity similar to that displayed by the Trump camp. One friend of mine confessed something to the order of, "I hate Trump. I don't like that I feel that way because I don't hate people. But I hate Trump."

Love the Sinner, Hate the Sin

As an advocate of LGBTQ rights and the view that homosexuals don't "choose" to be gay but simply *are* gay, I never thought I would find myself appreciating, much less quoting, the call to love the sinner but hate the sin. This call has always seemed to me to be misguided at best and hypocritical at worst. It implies that we must take a posture of loving gay people while hating their gay actions in order to convert them from being gay, and thus never really loving gay people in the first place. Such a lack of tolerance can hardly be called love.

However, while I may believe people are born gay or straight, I don't believe anyone is born racist, patriarchal, xenophobic, ableist, heterosexist, or the like. It's not simply "in someone's nature" to hold prejudicial attitudes or act in a discriminatory fashion. So in terms of dealing with people who exhibit and possess these tendencies in today's culture, I think it's right that we strive to hate the sin but love the sinner. But even in this context, some nuance is required.

Individuals don't "choose" to look down upon people of a different race, see women as objects, or fear Muslims. People think, feel, and act in these sorts of ways because they have been taught to do so. They have been socially constructed to respond to "others" in the way they do. In the nature versus nurture debate, nurture wins the day in this case. So if preachers want to have an impact on transforming the church (and society) in the face of the hatred to which Donald Trump has given a national voice and that he has legitimized, we must find ways to love the sinners who have been constructed in the way they have, and hate the sin that has done the constructing.

Loving the sinner will require a sound theological understanding of the character of sin of which we speak. Too often the church talks about sins (plural) of the individual instead of sin (singular) as a power that has control of us, as Paul speaks of sin in Romans 6. This tendency manifests itself in the ways we progressive Christians focus on individual acts of oppressive hatred because of the immediacy of their impact. Any good medical provider, however, knows that if someone's skin is breaking out in a terrible rash, you have to treat the rash directly *and* treat the underlying cause. Our individual sins (including individual acts of oppression) derive from this corrupting power of sin that characterizes the human condition.

Donald Trump and his most avid, Alt-right type of supporters didn't invent discrimination. Dividing society into the haves and have-nots, the powerful and the weak, male and female, able and disabled, this religion and that, this race and that, and even "deplorables" and acceptables is an inherent part of society itself. In other words, the kinds of hatred we have seen in the Trump campaign and that we fear will grow stronger during Trump's time in office is rooted in hatred that is a part of the structural fabric of our culture. It is systemic *Sin* (capital *S*) that, albeit in different ways and to different degrees, victimizes both the oppressed and the oppressors. So we must love all those caught in the web of Sin (including those who perpetuate it and benefit from it) while hating the Sin that is the underlying cause for the many symptoms we see erupting on the epidermis of the United States these days.

Love Your Enemies

While preachers must condemn oppressive speech and actions if we are to be faithful to the gospel, we must do so in ways that don't condemn persons who speak and act in oppressive ways. To be sure, we must counter the speech and actions of such people, but all the while caring for their plight as well as for the plight they inflict on others by participating in a sinfulness of humanity that is much bigger than any expression of that sin. In other words, we must have Christian empathy for the decaying state of the souls of oppressors that results from the hateful attitudes in which they have been nurtured without letting that empathy in any way lead us to condoning, denying, or being silent about those attitudes.

Indeed, perhaps empathy begins with identification. Before we can effectively address the "sinners" we are to love, we must confess that we, like them, have our own brand of intolerance. We must repent of the stereotyped views we have of those who rallied around Trump, and admit we are part of "the elite" who have not understood or cared for their plight.

"Love Trumps Hate" echoes the call of Jesus to love our neighbors. During the campaign, this was a call to stand in solidarity as sisters and brothers with those who are victims of hatred and oppression, in contrast to the way Trump exploited and intensified the existing divisions of gender, ethnicity, religion, class, education, and ideology. And now that the election's over, we must continue to embrace Jesus' command to love not only our neighbors, but also our enemies. We must find ways to love the classist, racist, sexist, homophobic, Islamophobic "others" in order to transform the whole of our society for the better of all in our society.

Frankly, this is a lesson we should have long learned by now. In his 1958 *Stride Toward Freedom*, almost sixty years ago, Martin Luther King Jr. first described in detail the theory and practice involved in the Montgomery Bus Boycott of

1955–56. As part of his description of the boycott, King laid out the main principles of his philosophy and strategy of nonviolence as a mode of social transformation. Two of these principles recur in his later sermons, speeches, and writings throughout the Civil Rights Movement, and are especially relevant for our current discussion:

> A second basic fact that characterizes nonviolence is that it does not seek to defeat or humiliate the opponent, but to win his [sic] friendship and understanding. The nonviolent resister must often express his protest through noncooperation or boycotts, but he realizes that these are not ends themselves; they are merely means to awaken a sense of moral shame in the opponent. The end is redemption and reconciliation...

> A third characteristic of this method is that the attack is directed against forces of evil rather than against persons who happen to be doing the evil. It is evil that the nonviolent resister seeks to defeat, not the person victimized by evil... We are out to defeat injustice and not white persons who may be unjust.[1]

King recognized that although they don't suffer to the same degree as the oppressed, oppressors are also victims of oppression who are in need of liberation from systemic oppression. Love toward oppressors, then, isn't demonstrated by some sentimental feeling, but by resisting participation in their oppression *in order to* free them from it. Oppressors are often unaware how much their lives are controlled by hate in trying to control the lives of others.

From a different socio-political context, Gustavo Gutiérrez makes the same type of argument as King. Writing out of concern for the poor in Latin American, this liberation theologian also argues for a love of enemies that will convert and free the oppressor alongside the oppressed:

The universality of Christian love is only an abstraction unless it becomes concrete history, process, conflict; it is arrived at only through particularity. To love all men and women does not mean avoiding confrontation; it does not mean preserving a fictitious harmony. Universal love is that which in solidarity with the oppressed seeks also to liberate the oppressors from their own power, from their ambition, and from their selfishness... One loves the oppressors by liberating them from themselves. But this cannot be achieved except by resolutely opting for the oppressed, that is, by combatting the oppressive class. It must be a real and effective combat, not hate. This is the challenge, as new as the gospel: to love our enemies... It is not a question of having no enemies, but rather of not excluding them from our love. But love does not mean that the oppressors are no longer enemies, nor does it eliminate the radicalness of the combat against them. "Love of enemies" does not ease tensions; rather it challenges the whole system and becomes a subversive formula.[2]

Many of us in the church "feel" the need to claim that we hate no one, that we have no enemies. But we can't love our enemies unless we admit that we have them. However, the real enemy is evil itself—oppression and hatred that infuses humanity. This infusion means that evil is an incarnate reality, just as are love, hope, mercy, and grace. So separating the evil from those perpetuating it is a difficult thing to do. The perspective proffered by King and Gutiérrez is absolutely necessary for a Christian approach to transforming the world and, in terms of our immediate concern, an appropriate theological and pastoral approach to preaching in response to the oppression and hate proffered by Trump and his supporters.

Preaching in the Enemy Camp

If we commit ourselves to preaching the gospel's radical ethic concerning peace, justice, and love for all, we are going to have to speak *about* Trump and his supporters as well as speak *to* Trump supporters.

This can be a frightening endeavor. Resistance to God's good news accompanied by a long practice of co-opting the gospel to support a self-serving status quo can lead to unhealthy and strident reactions when attempting to embrace the countercultural nature of the Christian life and Christian community. Preachers become vulnerable when they speak as prophets.

Yet our strategy isn't simply to speak the gospel, but to get the gospel heard, believed, and lived. Therefore, preaching the gospel's radical ethic concerning peace, justice, and love for all—not only in response to Trump and his supporters, but also directly to Trump supporters—is a great opportunity. Many mainline preachers dismiss the liturgical practice of offering invitations to conversion, but the current political reality calls us to re-embrace preaching for decision in a way that invites misogynists, racists, homophobes, and xenophobes to repent, be born again, and experience the freedom and joy of becoming a new creation.

If our prophetic tone is one of blame and shame, then such invitations won't be inviting. As we know, guilt and condemnation rarely inspire a new approach to life. We certainly need to speak honestly and clearly about the evil we are confronting, but the weight of the sermon needs to be on good news instead of the bad news. To use Eugene Lowry's language, every sermon needs to move from an itch to a scratch,[3] and the scratch must always be stronger than the itch.

In the "itch portion" of a prophetic sermon that intends to help liberate hearers from being trapped in the deadly cycle of oppression, the preacher must name and show the evil being addressed in ways that not only give hearers new tools for thinking about the problem, but also offer an *experience* of the evil they must reject and resist, even if they have embodied it in the past. As Michael Brothers has pointed out in his book *Distance in Preaching*, one way to do this is to create some distance between the hearer and the topic.[4] Instead of directly naming the ways hearers in the room have exhibited xenophobic attitudes and acted in xenophobic ways, we can provide examples of such attitudes and actions by others "out there," examples that even those who share the attitudes would experience as morally objectionable. Then, give the hearers room to make the connection to their own attitudes and actions instead of pounding the illustrations into them.

Another way to create an experience of the evil we want hearers to reject is to put a face on its victims. For most people, it's a lot easier to oppress someone or some group in the abstract than in the specific. A strategy often employed by the LGBTQ community is to forego arguments about nature versus nurture or the interpretation of biblical passages and instead show that the debate about homosexuality is about real human beings. Someone who is homophobic may feel no fear of or hatred for Lisa and her spouse, Mandy. Indeed, when someone hears the story of how they have been targeted just for loving each other, they may feel sympathy and grow to experience righteous indignation on their behalf.

Once an itch with some distance and perhaps a face on it has been created, preachers can lovingly nudge the hearers toward embracing a "scratch" that views strangers differently, leads toward a new ethic in dealing with strangers, and offers liberation from fearing the other. Distance can still be the preacher's friend in this portion of the sermon. Instead of using imperatives and telling hearers that they ought to think, feel, or do such-and-such, the preacher can tell a story of someone (or some community) moving from despising strangers to embracing the stranger. Showing is always more inviting than telling.

Because we are taking a cumulative approach to dealing with social issues raised during the era of Trump, not all of our stories in the scratch portion of sermons need to be grand tales to offer meaningful experiences. They simply need to be real.

You can tell the story of a congregation that decided to offer sanctuary to an immigrant who was going to be deported.

You can tell of the congregation so concerned about talking of radical Islamic terrorists while knowing so little about Islam that they invited a group of Muslims to lead a Q&A session at the church, and how that session led to an open dialogue between the local church and the local mosque.

You can tell the story of a white, teenage girl who was so inspired after visiting an African American worship service she wanted to visit a Chinese service and a Hispanic one.

You can tell the story of the prayer vigil in a small town in Indiana that, on the night of 9/11, included prayers for the victims, prayers for justice, and prayers for peace offered by Protestant, Catholic, Muslim, and Jewish clergy and laity.

You can tell of a college student's study abroad that changed not only his view of the world but also his theology and sense of vocation, leading him to change his major from business to religious studies and international affairs.

Given the use of social media in the 2016 campaign, you can even tell of something as simple as a Reddit thread in which people debated whether Trump's suggestion to register Muslims was ultimately about fear of Islam or not.[5] In the discussion were voices defending Trump's position, including one that explained that, in their view, the issue wasn't really religion anyway. To this person, the proposal was about registering people from Muslim-majority countries, so even a Christian Syrian refugee would have to register. Another person responded, "Let's flood the registry with Methodist Muslims, Baptism Muslims, Lutheran Muslims, Pentecostal Muslims, Anabaptist Muslims, etc." And then, echoing Martin Niemöller's statement condemning silence in the face of Nazi violence, the respondent concluded, "First they came for the Muslims, and we said, NOT THIS TIME."

Wouldn't it be wonderful if this happened? If we have learned our history lesson, it may be different this time. And wouldn't it be great if the ecumenical church that, in the past, has participated in the oppression of others *this* time banded together for their protection?

Wouldn't it be great this time if the church decided to be the church?

CHAPTER 6

Making the Church Great Again

As I asserted in the last chapter, preachers should demonize neither Donald Trump nor those who support him as they deal with social issues that arise as part of Trump's approach to running the country. That said, pastors are called by God to preach in ways that show offering anything less than a full and definitive condemnation of Trump's hateful rhetoric in order to keep it from becoming American policy is being unfaithful to Christ's proclamation of the reign of God.

But this isn't just a call for preachers; it's a gift. Yes, you read correctly: Trump's blatant prejudice and intended forms of discrimination is a gift of sorts to the church. Even while the possible institutionalizing of the bigotry he expresses is horrific to imagine, the threat is a gift that invites the church to be the church again. This is a moment in which God is offering the church a chance to engage in God's eschatological vision for the world. It is a chance for the church to cast aside its complacency and pick up the work of transforming the world instead of being conformed to it. It is a chance for preachers to reclaim the ethical voice that is the inheritance of the pulpit. It is a chance for us to *make the church great again.*

Ecclesiological Complicity

The idea of "making the church great again" implies there was a time when it was, in fact, great. In truth, I would be misrepresenting our history if I asserted that. There was no classical time in which the church wasn't in some way complicit with corrupt, oppressive political forces. Ever since Constantine legalized Christianity, the church and society have been united in marriage in the West. This marriage has at times been a happy one and at times a dysfunctional one; but, a marriage it has been. Referring to the relationship of the two as "Christendom" hasn't been an exaggeration.

Many would claim Christendom no longer exists in the United States. In the first place, we have never had a state church. We have from the beginning of our history held as sacred ideals the freedom of religion and the separation of church and State. Second, the moral and theological influence of the church has waned over the course of the twentieth century—as seen in the repealing of blue laws, the resistance to God-language in public discourse, consistently shrinking worship attendance, the loosening of restrictions concerning language and sexuality in the media, the schedule of youth sports claiming Sunday mornings, and the like.

Still, one only needs to count the number of American flags in Christian churches to recognize the marriage is still in place. The American flag and the Christian flag standing on either side of the altar table look like the bride and groom standing ever at the chancel announcing their vows to one another. It is certainly appropriate for Christians to love their country and, in secular settings, to pledge their allegiance to the flag. Christians can (and should?) be patriots. But it is another thing altogether for the flag to stand overshadowing the cross in the place where we worship the one and only God and claim to be citizens of God's reign. It's not hyperbole to say that this act is the most explicit example of idolatry in the church today.

One church in Kentucky had a tall flagpole in front of the church building where you entered the sanctuary. At the top of the pole was a huge American flag, and flying under it was a much smaller Christian flag. Then, on the church sign at the bottom of the flagpole, were the words, "Man [*sic*] cannot serve two masters." Unaware of the irony of the conflict between the implicit message of the flags and the explicit content on the sign, this church serves as a perfect example of the contemporary church's complicity with society. The church and the state are married, but the relationship is no longer one in which the church is a major influence on society or even where the two partners are equals. The church seems to have promised not only to love but also to obey its mate, and the result is an unconscious but very strong civil religion.

We preachers have allowed this situation to persist in our congregations and denominations. We've allowed the church to forget that it is to be, by its very definition, a counter-cultural movement. While this is by no means a new phenomenon, we should note how easy a posture this has been for progressive ministers to assume over the course of the last eight years. We said to ourselves, "Look how far we've progressed as a country since the days of slavery, Jim Crow, and the resistance to the Civil Rights Movement." Even though not successful on all fronts, Obama and his administration went on to champion many social causes we care about: health care for all, women's rights, human rights around the world, repair of the environment as a result of climate change, a nuanced approach to violence in and related to the Middle East, and compassion for immigrants. Since things in our world seemed better at least in terms of talk coming from the President, our sermons could focus on spiritual instead of political matters, individual instead of cultural issues.

But then came "the Donald." Not only was the U.S. not ready to elect a woman, we elected a man who promises to make America great again by taking us back to a day when greatness was defined in terms of whiteness. We elected one who bragged about being able to grope and force kisses on women because he was a celebrity. We elected one who argued that a successful approach to being greedy made him competent to be president. We elected one who promises to build a wall to keep Mexicans, who are "rapists and drug dealers," out of the country. We elected one who tweets insults at 3:00 a.m. about anyone who challenges him. We elected one who speaks about radical Islamic terrorism abroad to provoke fear of Muslim Americans in our own borders. We elected one who "drained the swamp" of politically trained civil servants to fill his cabinet with mostly white business men who possess more money than a third of American households combined. We elected Donald Trump because he and his campaign did a masterful job of making our anxieties and prejudices the primary issues of the campaign.

And now women's rights are threatened. Concern for racial equality is at risk. The well-being of Muslims and Latino/as is diminished. The poor in need of aid, including but not limited to health insurance, are more vulnerable than ever.

All of this is to say that Donald Trump has unintentionally been a vehicle for a divine gift igniting the church to say, "No more silence!" and preachers can say, "Let's get started being the church...again!"

Both/And

I'm not arguing that pastors need to forsake care of the individual soul in our preaching and focus solely on social justice issues. I have recently argued that preachers must deal cumulatively with three dimensions of the human condition:

- the vertical dimension involving our broken relationship with God,

- the horizontal dimension involving our broken relationship with others, and

- the inner dimension involving our broken relationship with ourselves.[1]

We don't preach only salvation in terms of the first and third dimensions, *or* only preach ethics in terms of the second dimension. We must preach both ethics and salvation, recognizing that salvation is ethical in nature and ethics are salvific in nature. The election of Donald Trump hasn't changed this—preachers must continue to address the whole of the human condition.

The advent of the era of Trump does, however, mean that we need to emphasize the horizontal dimension of the church's ethical outlook and activity in ways we haven't been doing or haven't been doing as strongly in the past as we must now. There is an urgency to the current state of affairs that calls preachers to reclaim the proclamation of God's eschatological reign of peace and justice to activate the church to keep the state of affairs from devolving as far as they might if Trump keeps his campaign promises. The radical and dangerous nature of President-elect Trump's rhetoric is a horrible "gift," allowing—nay, *urging*—preachers to let go of any reluctance they might have had about dealing with social issues in the pulpit in the past. While there never really was one, Trump has in the most striking fashion removed any valid excuse for preaching that fails to look outside the walls of the church.

Moreover, Trump has gifted us with the recognition that the way many of us have looked outside our walls in the past will not do. The church has too often been satisfied with offering the world its charity instead of working *in* the world for social change: sponsoring a food drive instead of addressing the causes of poverty; taking up collections for college scholarships for Native Americans without ever meeting a Native American; giving to a pastor's discretionary fund during communion to help people who have lost jobs due to a changing economy without investing in job training.

Mind you, almsgiving is an honored part of our religious tradition, and charity is indispensable to the work of the church. But the problem is that usually charity is the *end* of the church's mission instead of the *beginning*. Charity makes the giver feel good about doing good, but acts of charity should always serve to point the church toward deeper levels of engagement to bring about social change.

One of the most blatant examples of charity corrupting the fuller work of the church is the so-called "mission" trips churches sponsor so often. Indeed, a quick Google search will demonstrate that such trips have become quite a money-making industry. These are rarely (any more) grassroots events, and more often commercially sponsored forms of Christian tourism. They rarely lead to more significant forms of Christian mission.

Consider the example of one group of United Methodists that travels annually from the U.S. to El Salvador—not to join the poor in their struggle for justice and well-being, to help establish a clean water system, or even to help erect a permanent school or church building. They travel down to Central America, buy food, and get satisfaction by passing it out to the poor in person. It is a Christian shopping extravaganza. Oh, to see a poor, old woman's brown face light up when a white man hands her two oranges! The *gracias* made it all worthwhile!

There is little self-reflection among the First World sponsors or participants of the group to admit that if, instead of traveling to Central America, they just sent the money for the food *and* the money they spent on their own travel, lodging, and food, the people would have much more food. It would be a more significant level of charity. Beyond that, there is no apparent awareness in the group of the ways charity without social action perpetuates the social ills that keep poor people impoverished, as opposed to being their allies as they seek to claim a more secure status and stable level of well-being in society. To do this, however, would require that the mission team give up much (all?) of their own status, recognizing the hubris of their actions and the self-serving nature of their endeavors.

The Gospel of Luke is clear that the oppressed can only be lifted up when the oppressor is brought down. In the Magnificat, for instance, Mary prophesies that God

> has shown strength with his arm;
> he has scattered the proud in the thoughts of
> their hearts.
> He has brought down the powerful from their
> thrones, and lifted up the lowly;
> he has filled the hungry with good things,
> and sent the rich away empty. (1:51–53)

Similarly, in the Beatitudes, Luke doesn't present Jesus blessing the "poor in spirit" the way Matthew does (Mt. 5:3), but, instead: "Blessed are you who are poor," and, "Woe to you who are rich" (Lk. 6:20, 24).

President-elect Trump has proclaimed a gospel of blessed are the rich, the white, the able-bodied, the male, the celebrity, the straight, and the evangelical. He has promised future blessings that are a reclamation of past privilege (accompanied by past levels of oppression). And in doing so, he has gifted the church with the chance to say we will no longer be satisfied with being God's Band-aid on the social ills of the world. We will increase our charity, but we will also take up the challenge of engaging in mission that aims at changing the structures that make charity necessary.

Preaching Mission

In order to preach mission that will counter Trumpian values, three broad homiletical strategies will be especially helpful to pastors.

First, we must make room in our sermons and our liturgies for *confession and lament.* We must be honest with ourselves and with God. We must confess the role that the church played in the bigotry and anxiety that got the likes of a Donald Trump elected. We can't pretend to be the holy community of faith taking on the sinful world. We are both in and of the sins of the world in this case. Confession is best served with lament. We must find faith to challenge God in these times, asking why God allows hatred, ignorance, and oppression to set the agenda for this era. The psalms are a rich homiletical and liturgical resource for this strategy.

The second strategy has to do with preaching ecclesiology *in declarative terms instead of imperatives*. When preachers tell the church what they need to be doing, the congregation hears the negative flip side: "You're not doing what you are supposed to." More than inspiring or challenging, imperatives usually evoke guilt or shame. Congregations experience sermons of this sort the same way children experience a parent chastising them for not doing as they were supposed to do, and saying, "I'm not angry at you; I'm disappointed in you." Heads lower so as not to make eye contact.

Instead of preachers calling the church to become *who we ought to be* (ethically speaking), we should name *who the church is* (theologically speaking). We should speak of mission, reminding hearers that mission is who we are (instead of who we ought to be). People will want to live up to that which defines them. Their heads will be raised (meeting the preacher's eyes) with a sense of pride and purpose, saying, "You know, that *is* who we are! Let's get moving."

In other words, when we tell a congregation who they are in declarative sentences, they will turn them into self-claimed imperatives. Of course, this doesn't happen in one sermon. We must preach this ecclesiological definition repeatedly in nuanced ways for it to take hold. To be effective in doing this, we must *show* them the church defined as mission and not simply tell them. We must provide imagery of individuals and congregations that are involved in mission. The images may be taken from other communities of faith, but we still claim them as defining who we are.

A third homiletical strategy needed to help the progressive church become a mission-active church is to preach *eschatology*. We moderns and postmoderns have, to a great extent, left eschatology in the wake of our progress. We often think of eschatology as being prominent in the prophets and the Book of Revelation, but the early Christian movement was thoroughly eschatological. I would dare say that *every* page of the New Testament includes eschatological themes and language that we miss from our scientific-worldview perch positioned two thousand years away. We don't sit at our windows waiting for Christ to come surfing in on the clouds, so we miss the more subtle elements of the eschatological outlook that is part of who we are.

For the early church, the Christ event (in the past) was an eschatological event. The cross and resurrection marked a turning of the ages. That means the church lives in the last days. That statement need not be taken literally to still be claimed faithfully. The last days are characterized by an "already/not yet" perspective. *We* have *already* experienced the salvation revealed in Jesus Christ and live in the light of that good news. However, *the world* has *not yet* experienced that good news manifested throughout the whole of creation.

To help contemporary ears understand the ancient eschatological outlook, I often use the illustration of being in a car on a two-lane country road at night. There are few street lights in such a setting, so we turn on our high beams and perhaps edge closer to the center of the road to be safe. Then, driving up a hill, we notice headlights shining over the top of the hill from the other direction. What do we do? We move back to the right, away from the center line, and turn our lights down. That moment is the eschatological experience. We have *already* experienced enough of the other car to have changed our behavior, but have *not yet* seen the car fully revealed.

We in the church have *already* experienced God's love, grace, justice, peace, and calling on our lives, and *yet* the world still struggles with violence, suffering, lack of resources, hatred, inequality, and so on and so forth. We are perpetually driving up that hill celebrating what we have experienced of God while being utterly dissatisfied with the state of the world. Having experienced a sliver of God's character, we know something of God's vision for the whole of God's creation. Sharing God's dissatisfaction with the pain experienced in and by the world leads us to act in cooperation with God. What Paul advises of individuals fits also for the church engaged in missions:

> ...present your bodies as a living sacrifice, holy and acceptable to God, which is your spiritual worship. Do not be conformed to this world, but be transformed by the renewing of your minds, so that you may discern what is the will of God—what is good and acceptable and perfect (Rom. 12:1b–2).

The eschatological church properly defined can't and won't be satisfied to conform to the world, but will be transformed by the renewing of our minds to discern and do God's will in striving to transform the world.

PART II

PULPIT STRATEGIES

In the previous pages, I have examined the beginning of the Trump era and what I see as the church's and preachers' appropriate responses to it from a range of different theological angles.

In the material that follows, I turn my attention to specific social justice issues raised by views Trump expressed during the campaign and the early post-election days. The issues covered are not all of the social issues raised by Trump that should trouble the church. Instead, they are those in which he attacks specific groups of people.

Trump did not invent the kinds of bigotry and hatred he expressed during the election. The United States and the American church have been struggling with them since long before the last election cycle. Nevertheless, "The Donald" played the issues as one trump card after another to take as many tricks as possible without regard for standards of justice, civility, or compassion. Each chapter that follows, then, begins with a list of examples of ways Trump,

Trump's staff, Trump's supporters, and/or Trump's appointees give the vulnerable in our society cause to fear that the social issues will become more intense during Trump's time in office. Readers may be tempted to scan through or even skip over these lists, but I'd urge you to take some time with them. Even though you are likely familiar with most of the incidents included, it is important that we not let them fade into the past. The cumulative effect of reading them together reminds preachers of long-running patterns of oppressive speech and action by Trump, and of the high stakes we face in the coming days.

Following the opening list, we turn away from Trump and focus on the issue itself for the bulk of the chapter. The main focus is not to analyze in any exhaustive manner the social issues being discussed. I strongly recommend that preachers read sociologists, political scientists, theologians, and social ethicists who are better scholars on these issues than I. My contribution, I hope, is simply to offer a few framing thoughts about the various matters as they relate to preaching, and then to offer a few suggestions (and at times caveats) in relation to dealing with the topics in the pulpit. I don't intend the list of strategies I present to be exhaustive. Instead, they are meant to be suggestive, so that preachers choose some, reject some, adapt some, and add others to them.

CHAPTER 7

Race

Examples of Trump's racism in general:

- The Justice Department sued The Trump Management Corporation for alleged racial discrimination against African Americans looking to rent apartments in Brooklyn, Queens, and Staten Island (1973).[1]

- As U.S. attorney, Jeff Sessions (Trump's nominee for Attorney General) prosecuted three African American civil rights activists for voter fraud due to their role in helping poor, uneducated, and often illiterate Black voters mark their ballots with their permission. The jury acquitted the defendants after only three hours of deliberation (1985).[2]

- According to John O'Donnell, Trump said, "I've got black accountants at Trump Castle and Trump Plaza. Black guys counting my money! I hate it... The only kind of people I want counting my money are short guys that wear yarmulkes every day." O'Donnell also recounts Trump referring to an African American employee, saying, "I think the guy is lazy. And it's probably not his fault because laziness is a trait in blacks. It really is, I believe that. It's not anything they can control" (1991).[3]

- The New Jersey Casino Control Commission fined the Trump Plaza Hotel and Casino $200,000 because managers were removing African American card dealers at the request of some big-spending gamblers (1992).[4]

- When Trump wanted to open a casino in Bridgeport, Connecticut, that would compete with one owned by the Mashantucket Pequot Nation, he testified before the House subcommittee on Native American Affairs and said of those running the casino, "They don't look like Indians to me... They don't look like Indians to Indians" (1993).[5]

- Trump became a leading voice in questioning whether President Obama was born in the United States, even to the point of asserting that he sent personal investigators to Hawaii (2011).[6]

- Trump announced his run for the presidency and said, "When Mexico sends its people, they're not sending their best. They're not sending you. They're sending people that have lots of problems, and they're bringing those problems with them. They're bringing drugs. They're bringing crime. They're rapists. And some, I assume, are good people" (June 16, 2015).[7]

- When two brothers were arrested in Boston for beating up a homeless Latino man and said to the police, "Donald Trump was right—all these illegals need to be deported," Trump responded, "I will say that people who are following me are very passionate. They love this country and they want this country to be great again. They are passionate" (Aug. 21, 2015).[8]

- During a campaign speech, Trump did an impression of Asian negotiators, using broken English: "When these people walk into the room," Trump began. "They don't say, 'Oh hello, how's the weather? It's so beautiful outside. How are the Yankees doing? They're doing wonderful, that's great.' They say, 'We want deal!'" (Aug. 26, 2015).[9]

- At a Trump campaign rally, Trump supporters physically attacked an African-American protester, including kicking him while he was on the ground, after the man began chanting, "Black lives matter." The following day, Trump said, "Maybe [the protester] should have been roughed up," he mused. "It was absolutely disgusting what he was doing" (Nov. 22, 2015).[10]

- Donald Trump retweets a Photoshopped picture of Jeb Bush holding up a sign saying, "Vote Trump" that was originally tweeted by white supremacist, @ WhiteGenocideTM (Jan. 22, 2016). Throughout his campaign Trump retweeted white supremacist tweets that praised him.[11]

- Trump refuses to denounce endorsement adamantly by former KKK leader, David Duke (Feb. 28, 2016).[12]

- Trump called federal judge Gonzalo Curiel a "hater" who was biased in his judgments against him in the ongoing class action suit accusing Trump University of fraud because he is "Hispanic" and "Mexican" (even though the judge was born in Indiana) (June 2, 2016).[13] Immediately after winning the general election, Trump settled the case for $25 million (Nov. 18, 2016).[14]

- Trumped tweeted a picture of Hilary Clinton in front of piles of money with a Star of David and the words, "Most corrupt candidate ever" (July 2, 2016).[15]

- Trump appointed Stephen Bannon, executive chair of Breitbart News, as the CEO of his campaign (Aug 17, 2016) and Chief White House Strategist (Nov. 13, 2016). Under Bannon's editorial direction, Breitbart published stories with the following headlines: "Bill Kristol: Republican spoiler, renegade Jew," "Birth control makes women unattractive and crazy," "Would you rather your child had feminism or cancer?" and "Gay rights have made us dumber, it's time to get back in the closet."[16]

- Donald Trump Jr. reposted an Instagram meme that Photoshopped an image of Trump and a number of his supporters (including Donald Jr., conspiracy theorist Alex Jones, and Milo Yiannopoulos, who was banned from Twitter for his hate-inciting rhetoric) that included Pepe the Frog, a cartoon character used by Alt-right members in propaganda supporting racism, anti-Semitism, and white Nationalism (Sept. 11, 2016).[17]

- During a campaign speech, Donald Trump said, "Our African American communities are absolutely in the worst shape that they've ever been in before—ever, ever, ever. You take a look at the inner cities, you get no education, you get no jobs, you get shot walking down the street" (Sept. 20, 2016).[18]

- At a campaign rally, Trump used standard anti-Semitic language warning that Hillary Clinton "meets in secret with international banks to plot the destruction of U.S. sovereignty" and that "a global power structure" was conspiring against ordinary Americans (on Oct. 13, 2016). Three weeks later, Trump released one of the final television ads of his campaign, repeating language from that speech while showing pictures of several well-known Jews: George

Soros (financier), Janet Yellen (Federal Reserve Chair), and Lloyd Blankfein (Goldman Sachs CEO) (Oct. 13, 2016).[19]

- At an Alt-right celebration of Trump's victory, Richard Spencer offered the closing speech, which included Nazi propaganda. As members of the audience stood and made the Nazi salute, Spencer shouted, "Hail Trump! Hail our People! Hail victory! [a translation of *Seig Heil*]." (Nov. 19, 2016).[20]

- President-elect Trump chose Jeff Sessions to serve as Attorney General, a position held by two African Americans over the course of the last eight years. In the past, the Senate would not approve Sessions for a federal judgeship due to allegations that he had called a Black attorney "boy" and suggested that a white attorney working for Black clients was a race traitor.[21]

Getting a Handle on the Church's Racism

The history of the United States is a history of racism. European colonists and their descendants have oppressed persons of Native American, African, Asian, Jewish, and Latin American heritage and their descendants from our earliest days on. There has been no time when white racism was not a serious factor in our society.

Many Americans have hoped that racism's hold on our culture was (finally) waning. After all, there is much celebration of pluralism and diversity in the postmodern age, and the country elected its first African American president in 2008, and re-elected him in 2012! At the very least, the most blatant racists seemed to have gone underground and most forms of racism were expressed in a more subtle fashion.

But we were naïve. During the past election racist themes were repeatedly named and—even more often—implied by Donald Trump. And having found a racist spokesperson in place to run the country, racist groups who claim Trump as their champion have felt emboldened and legitimized by his election. Segments of the Ku Klux Klan in North Carolina held a rally and named their plans to have a parade celebrating Trump's victory.[22] Bill O'Reilly of Fox News has explicitly criticized the left for wanting "power taken away from the white establishment" and for "arguing that white privilege in America [is] an oppressive force that must be done away with."[23] Alt-right and white nationalists are already considering candidates who will explicitly carry their agenda forward whom they may want to run in federal elections in 2018.[24]

Fear among minorities is rightfully widespread. A telling example that was shared with me is that after the election, one African American elementary-aged child in Atlanta asked her teacher if "they" were going to make "us" slaves again. While adults know such an action would never happen, mature persons of color are realistic in recognizing that economic, cultural, verbal, and physical forms of violence can (and likely will) experience a significant statistical rise that will threaten their individual and communal well-being. And they know that Trump's administration is primed to institute policies to diminish the strides of affirmative action in education and business and allow for racial profiling in law enforcement and the justice system. In other words, they expect to hear voices protesting and to experience the wrath of white Americans who protest that Black [and Brown] lives don't matter.

As with the country, the history of the American church is a history of racism. To our shame, we've often done more to keep racist structures in place than to tear them down. To be fair, we've had moments of which we can be proud, moments in U.S. history when segments of the church fought for racial equality in culture and in the church. But these have been too few and too far between.

On April 17, 1960, Martin Luther King Jr. appeared on *Meet the Press* and said his famous line: "I think it is... one of the shameful tragedies of our nation that 11:00 on Sunday mornings is one of the most segregated hours, if not the most segregated hour, in Christian America. And any church that...has a segregated body is standing against the spirit and the teachings of Jesus Christ and fails to be a true witness."[25] Since that day, our appreciation of the ways communal identity is formed has become nuanced so that we now value culturally distinct religious communities in a way we could not when African Americans were having to fight for the basic civil rights of racial minorities (see the chapter "Us and Them," above). That said, the underlying racism of many American congregations and denominations pointed out in King's indictment of the church is still evident. The church should lead the country in dismantling racism, but in truth the church has usually followed the country as a soldier in its racist army. Indeed, Donald Trump was elected with the votes of many church members across the country.

Preaching about Racism

How does the preacher step up to the pulpit to address issues of race in the situation? Preachers of color need to continue to claim or reclaim the prophetic voices of civil rights preachers while being informed by progress in liberation and ethnic theologies that have developed in the last half-century. Preaching on race, however, must not be left to congregations that are victims of racism. As a white preacher myself, I don't have the experience, expertise, or right to offer specific homiletical strategies for preaching in Black, Hispanic, or Asian congregations. So in what follows in this chapter, the homiletical context I primarily have in mind is worship in predominantly white congregations where issues of race discrimination need to be addressed with urgency due to Trump's race baiting and the worsening racial situation in our society.

White preachers especially have a problem—surrounded by racism, benefitting from white privilege, and unconsciously participating in racist structures—when they try to preach to a racist congregation in a racist culture. The first difficulty is, of course, helping the white church see and admit the ways it has been and continues to be racist. Many in the church are comfortable agreeing that the woman in a JC Penney store who went on a tirade against a Hispanic shopper in line is racist,[26] but *my friend and I,* who voted to make America great again, aren't. Many of us have a far too narrow definition of racism, and the beginning point for preachers who want to address it is to help congregations widen the circle of who is included in the label "racist."

I remember, back when I was in school, I attended a United Methodist Men's retreat. A white man who taught sociology of religion at an African American seminary said to us without blinking, "If you are a white male raised in the South [which most of us were], you are racist. I am a racist. We can't help it. In fact, we can never completely escape it. But we can do something about it." My first response was to reject what he said completely. Indeed, *because* I had been raised in the South and had heard and seen so much racism as a youth, I abhorred racism. Others expressed the same sentiment. "It is good you hate racism," he said. "But it won't make much difference unless you admit that you hate something that is in you." He spent the weekend showing us ways we hold racist attitudes without knowing, ways situations can make stereotypes pop into our heads beyond our control, ways we live out of white privilege without recognizing that we're doing so. It was an enlightening (albeit painful) weekend for me, and decades since then I continue to recognize and struggle with ways I benefit from being white in a racist society.

My daughter started driving a few years ago. My wife and I taught her how to be a defensive driver, to obey the laws, to pass an eighteen-wheeler on the highway, and to (ugh!) parallel park. Around that time there was a beating of yet another unarmed, young African American by a police officer during a traffic stop. On the news, we watched Black parents describe how, as part of teaching their teenage children to drive, they had to teach them to behave when "driving while Black" in case they were pulled over by an officer. They feared for their children's lives at the hands of the very police forces to whom we entrusted our daughter's life. My wife and I looked at each other, hating to admit at this moment we were glad our daughter was white and feeling pain over the fact that some parents had worries for their teenager's safety on a daily basis that went far beyond anything we could imagine.

Helping white congregations redefine racism in relation to *structures* that shape both the oppressed and the oppressor, and not just in terms of disparate, individual actions—in ways that they can acknowledge their own individual and corporate prejudice and racism, even if they do not hold racist intentions—will lead many of them to want to do something about those structures. If a white preacher reveals the systemic racism prevalent throughout the church and society with a tone of confession (that is, acknowledging her or his own participation in, and being trapped by, racist structures), others will let their defenses down at the accusation of being "racists" and be able to travel with the preacher in a way they could not if the preacher speaks of racists only in the second and third person.

Put differently, the first step to recovery is admitting we have a problem. Perhaps, analogous to addicts, there is no such thing as a former racist. At best, persons of European descent in America can be recovering racists: we actively resist our bent toward racism, taking it one day at a time, and inviting others into the program. Before a church can "work the program," our hearers have to admit that racism is a problem in the world, in our country, in our local culture, in our church, and in ourselves.

A second homiletical strategy to employ in addressing racism is to recognize biblical texts that invite preachers to touch on the subject.

The Bible is filled with texts that invite preachers to bring racism into a sermon. In ancient scripture, race (in terms of a construct of dividing people by skin color) was not the issue it is today. However, dividing people along similar lines was. Discriminating on the basis of ethnicity was. The early narratives of Genesis that begin to describe whence different nations came, to the enslavement of the Israelites in Egypt, the conquests of Canaanite and Philistine lands and people by the Israelites, the prophetic oracles describing God's and Israel's relations with different nations, the early Jewish and Christian views of Samaritans in the Gospels and Acts, and the division between Gentile and Jewish Christians in the early church, all invite commentary on contemporary racial oppression.

A third homiletical strategy that grows out of the previous one is that the central claim of a sermon need not be about racism for preachers to lift up issues related to structural racism in a sermon. Indeed, bringing racism into sermons dealing with other topics will normalize the discussion a great deal. Just naming an ethnic division in a biblical text that is similar to racial divides in today's world and then moving on to a different element of the text that will be a homiletical major focus normalizes the discussion of race in the church.

This is not to say that we don't need to preach full sermons focusing on racism. We absolutely do. But sermons here or there on racism are not enough. The white church needs to find ways to have *ongoing* conversations about race that will change the way we as the body of Christ think, talk, and act in the United States.

A fourth homiletical strategy suggested by the discussion above concerning normalizing the discussion of racism is the need in our sermons to "normalize" race, if you will. In our sermonic imagery, we preachers need to make sure we use people of different racial and ethnic identities than the dominant racial and ethnic identity of the congregation. We need to make sure that white listeners don't always picture white persons when we say, "A woman at the office," "a child in the park," etc. When we use persons of color as positive characters in stories (as opposed to only referring to them when we are discussing them in the context of discussing racism), we invite white hearers to identify with them and learn from them as opposed to seeing them only as different from "us."

On the other hand, we must be careful not just to throw "an African American man" into our sermon stories every once in a while. If white preachers usually tell stories with an introduction similar to, "The other day I saw a woman in the grocery store," and say, "The other day I saw a Latina in the grocery store," even though the character's ethnicity plays no role in the story, this tokenizes persons of color and implies that white is the norm. This practice can have the patronizing and rationalizing sound of "Some of my best friends are Black." The unintended effect is to reveal my bias even though I am trying to show my inclusivity.

———————

In the era of Trump, racism is on the rise and political correctness is seen as an obstacle instead of an ethic. And old justifications for racism are rising with it: the need for "law and order," national security, and protection of jobs. When Bull Connor turned fire hoses and attack dogs on

African American protestors in Birmingham, many churches were silent. Will we be silent again in the face of presidential calls to support police policies such as stop and frisk without critical oversight that looks for racism behind the practice? When Japanese Americans were placed in internment camps during World War II (even though German Americans were not), many churches said nothing. Will we be silent again in the face of presidential actions to register all Muslims and refuse refugees from Muslim countries? When Irish immigrants were stereotyped as being lazy and drunkards and told "Irish need not apply," many churches did nothing. Will we still do nothing when Latin American immigrants are stereotyped not just as lazy, but as rapists and drug dealers and deserving of mass deportation? There is nothing new under the sun, but churches should recognize the return of these motifs as antithetical to the gospel and should act quickly in the Trump era.

CHAPTER 8

Gender

Examples of Trump's sexism toward women in general:

- Trump said of the media, "You know, it doesn't really matter what [they] write as long as you've got a young and beautiful piece of a**" (1991).[1]

- In an interview with *New York Magazine,* Trump said of women, "You have to treat 'em like s***" (1992).

- Swedish model Vendela Kirsebom claims that at the White House Correspondents' Dinner Trump spent the evening commenting on and comparing the breasts and legs of women in the room (1993).[2]

- In an interview with ABC News, Trump named expectations of his wife, who at the time was Marla Maples: "I have days where, if I come home—and I don't want to sound too much like a chauvinist, but when I come home and dinner's not ready, I go through the roof." Later in the interview, he named how he gets bored with women once they're successful: "I think that putting a wife to work is a very dangerous thing. Unfortunately, after they're a star, the fun is over for me. It's like a creation process. It's almost like creating a building. It's pretty sad" (1994).

- In his book, *Trump: The Art of the Comeback,* Trump comments on prenuptial agreements: "There are basically three types of women and reactions. One is the good woman who very much loves her future husband, solely for himself, but refuses to sign the agreement on principle. I fully understand this, but the man should take a pass anyway and find someone else. The other is the calculating woman who refuses to sign the prenuptial agreement because she is expecting to take advantage of the poor, unsuspecting sucker she's got in her grasp. There is also the woman who will openly and quickly sign a prenuptial agreement in order to make a quick hit and take the money given to her" (1997).

- In an interview with the *Daily News,* Trump claimed all the women on *The Apprentice* flirted with him "consciously or unconsciously" (2004).

- Trump tweeted, "26,000 unreported sexual assaults [*sic*] in the military—only 238 convictions. What did these geniuses expect when they put men & women together?" (2013).

- A 2005 *Entertainment Tonight* video that was leaked, in which Trump is speaking to Billy Bush on a bus, most explicitly reveals his nature as a sexual predator. It opens with Trump admitting that he was unable to bed ("I did try and f**k her... I moved on her like a b***h.") an unnamed, married woman. As the bus arrives for Trump's cameo appearance on *Days of Our Lives,* Bush comments on the looks of the woman waiting to accompany Trump. Trump responds, "I better use some Tic Tacs just in case I start kissing her. You know I'm automatically attracted to beautiful—I just start kissing them. Just kiss. I don't even wait. And when you're a star, they let you do it. You can do anything. Grab 'em by the p***y. You can do anything" (Oct 7, 2016).

Examples of Trump's sexist verbal attacks/comments directed at specific women:

- Trump commented on Katrina Witt, German gold-medal Olympic ice skater, saying, "Wonderful looking while on the ice, but up close and personal, she could only be described as attractive if you like a woman with a bad complexion who is built like a linebacker" (1992).[3]

- On *The Howard Stern Show,* Trump ranked famous women with whom he'd like to have sex. The list included: Melania Knauss (then his girlfriend, now wife), Ivana Trump (his first wife), Princess Diana, Michelle Pfeiffer, Cameron Diaz, Julia Roberts, Cindy Crawford, Mariah Carey, Gwyneth Paltrow, and Diane Sawyer (2000).

- On *The Howard Stern Show,* Trump referred to his daughter Ivanka as "voluptuous" and then later on *The View* said, "If Ivanka weren't my daughter, perhaps I'd be dating her" (2006).

- Trump ranting against Rosie O'Donnell on *Entertainment Tonight:* "Rosie O'Donnell is disgusting, both inside and out. If you take a look at her, she's a slob. How does she even get on television? If I were running *The View,* I'd fire Rosie. I'd look her right in that fat, ugly face of hers and say, 'Rosie, you're fired...' We're all a little chubby, but Rosie's just worse than most of us... Rosie's a person who's very lucky to have her girlfriend. And she better be careful or I'll send one of my friends over to pick up her girlfriend;

why would she stay with Rosie if she had another choice?" (2006).

- Trump mailed Gail Collins a picture of herself with the words "the face of a dog" written across it after she wrote an article about rumors of his bankruptcy in *The New York Times* (2011).

- After Megyn Kelly asked Trump about referring to women as "fat pigs, dogs, slobs, and disgusting animals" in the first Republican primary debate, he called her a "bimbo" in a tweet and then went on in a CNN interview to say, "You could see there was blood coming out of her eyes. Blood coming out of her wherever" (Aug. 7, 2015). Nine months later, when Trump is interviewed by Megan Kelly, he responds to her naming that he called her a bimbo by saying, "Did I say that? Excuse me... Over your life, Megyn, you've been called a lot worse, wouldn't you say?" (May 18, 2016).

- During a debate, Clinton accused Trump of calling 1996 Miss Universe Alicia Machado "fat." Machado had said Trump had called her "Miss Piggy" and "Miss Housekeeping." After asking, in surprise, "Where did you find this?" Trump went on to say, "She was the winner and she gained a massive amount of weight, and it was a real problem for us." During the night after the debate, Trump posted a series of tweets attacking Machado. One a few days later was posted at 5:30 a.m.: "Did Crooked Hillary help disgusting (check out sex tape and past) Alicia M become a U.S. citizen so she could use her in the debate?" There is no evidence of the existence of any sex tape (Sept. 30, 2016).

Examples of Trump's sexist comments and behavior regarding female candidates:

- Trump re-tweeted a post saying, "If Hillary can't satisfy her husband what makes her think she can satisfy America?" (Apr. 16, 2015).

- Trump insulted fellow Republican candidate Carla Fiorina. In a *Rolling Stone* interview he said, "Look at that face. Would anyone vote for that? Can you imagine that, the face of our next president? I mean, she's a woman, and I'm not supposed to say bad things, but really, folks, come on. Are we serious?" (Sept. 9, 2015). Then, at a Republican debate in which all candidates were interrupting one another, Trump singled Fiorina out: "Why does she keep interrupting everybody?" (Nov. 10, 2015).

- During the first debate of the general election, Trump interrupted Clinton twenty-five times in the first twenty-six minutes, "mansplained" to her, and finally said of her, "She doesn't have the look. She doesn't have the stamina" (Sept. 26, 2016).

- Following a town hall debate in which Trump was accused of stalking and looming over Hillary Clinton, Trump, at a rally, blamed Clinton for walking in front of him, saying, "And when she walked in front of me, believe me, I wasn't impressed" (Oct. 14, 2016).

Examples of accusations of sexual assault against Trump:[4]

- According to Jessica Leeds, Donald Trump assaulted her on a plane, fondling her breasts and trying to reach under her skirt during a plane flight (1980).

- In 1997, makeup artist Jill Harth filed a lawsuit against Trump accusing him of cornering her and groping her in his daughter's bedroom four years earlier (1993).

- According to four contestants, Trump walked into the Miss USA Teen pageant contestants' dressing room without announcing himself (1997).

- Miss Utah, Temple Taggart, accused Donald Trump of forcing a kiss on the lips on two separate occasions during the Miss USA pageant (1997).

- Rachel Crooks, a receptionist working in Trump Tower, alleges Trump assaulted her in a Tower elevator by advancing from a handshake to a kiss on the check to a kiss on her lips, without her consent (2005).

- Natasha Stoynoff, a staff writer for *People*, claims that following an interview with Trump and his wife Melania, Trump gave her a private tour of his Mar-a-Lago estate, during which he pushed her against a wall, forcing his tongue down her throat (2005).

Here are more examples of Trump's history of sexist comments and actions:

- Carrie Prejean wrote about "the Trump rule" at the Miss USA pageant (co-owned by Trump), claiming that Trump had the contestants parade in front of him so he could separate those he found attractive from those he didn't (2009).

- Trump had men rate the appearance of women on *The Apprentice* (2010).

- When Brande Roderick was a contestant on *Celebrity Apprentice*, she knelt in front of Trump during a board meeting to ask him whether she could be the next project manager. Trump responded, "It must be a pretty picture— you dropping to your knees" (2013).

- According to Cassandra Searles, Miss Washington and Miss USA contestant, Trump grabbed her a** and invited her to his hotel room (2013).

- During the election, the Associated Press released comments from people who worked on *The Apprentice* revealing a culture of misogyny. Trump would rate female contestants on the basis of the size of their breasts and discussed with which ones he would like to have sex. Trump speculated about which female contestant would be "a tiger in bed." A crew member who asked not to be identified recalled: "We were in the boardroom one time figuring out who to blame for the task, and he just stopped in the middle and pointed to someone and said, 'You'd f**k her, wouldn't you? I'd f**k her. C'mon, wouldn't you?'" (Oct 3, 2016).

Sexual discrimination lawsuits against Trump and Trump companies:

- *USA Today* investigates over 4000 lawsuits against Trump and his companies, finding that twenty cases dating back as far as the 1980s reveal a pattern of alleged sexual discrimination in Trump organizations (Oct. 9, 2016).

Getting a Handle on the Church's Sexism

Since the beginning of human history, as far as we know, human culture has been primarily patriarchal. "Patriarchy" is defined as societal structures in which males possess more social and political power than females. The original source of patriarchy is likely found in the fact that male members of the human species generally have more physical strength than the female members. In the most ancient of days of our species, brute force was necessary for survival.

As human societies evolved, various forms of production and intellectual prowess were needed for the advancement of the species. Most of these did not depend on brute force, so that females could have participated in them equally with males. However, because the pattern of male dominance had already been established, along with a human (or male!) propensity for war—which, in its earliest days, did continue to depend primarily on physical strength—patriarchy and sexism continued to rule the day. "Sexism" can be defined as the belief that males are superior to females and the continued oppressive forms of patriarchy that result from such belief.

The United States is certainly heir to and perpetuator of this sexist heritage. From our beginning we have argued that all "men" are created equal, an ideal that excluded women in the beginning. Beginning in the late nineteenth century, American women began struggling for and slowly obtaining the rights due to them, beginning with the right to vote (gained in 1920). While patriarchy may have lessened, it is still very much with us. Hillary Clinton was the first woman to be nominated by a political party as its presidential candidate. Only forty-six women have ever served in the U.S. Senate. In the workplace, women make about seventy-nine cents for every dollar made by men. Women make up about 44 percent of employees in S&P 500 companies, but less than 10 percent of the top earners in the companies are female, and under 5 percent of these companies have women as CEOs.[5] Disparity of pay based on sex is even evident in Hollywood: female celebrities make significantly less than their male counterparts in television and film, and reach their earning peak at a much younger age due to the way the entertainment industry values appearance in relation to female age.[6]

The church's history parallels secular history in being a patriarchal and sexist institution. Men have shaped the theology and practices of the church in almost every era of its existence. For most of the church's history, women could not be ordained—the logic being: since Jesus and the apostles were men, only men could lead the church. Many evangelical traditions still do not allow for women to be ordained. And Pope Francis, for all of the commitments he has made to progress in relation to social justice issues, recently indicated he views the ban on ordination of women in the Roman Catholic Church as being permanent.[7] While

Mainline Protestant denominations on the whole do ordain women today, there still exists a serious stained-glass ceiling that keeps men at the top of the ecclesiastical pyramid, serving the majority of the larger churches and the majority of judicatory posts in denominations.

The church should lead the country in dismantling sexism and in the struggle for gender equality, but in truth the church has partnered with culture in keeping women "in their place." Indeed, Donald Trump was elected with the votes of many church members who agree with his objectifying view of women and think making America great again includes a traditional political, economic, and familial hierarchy with men at the top and women below.

Preaching about Sexism

How does the preacher step up to the pulpit to address gender issues in this situation? Women have pushed the church and society to be more inclusive and just in its perspective on and treatment of women, but this is an issue that all preachers, regardless of their gender, should be addressing.

The first homiletical strategy is to raise, honestly and explicitly, the issue of patriarchy in the world as something that is of concern to God and the church. The list of sexist and misogynist language and actions above should have led preachers during the election to talk about women's issues. When the pulpit is silent in the face of such blatant public sexism, the impression is that the church condones it. Women's issues are human issues are theological issues.

A second obvious strategy in dealing with patriarchy concerns the use of inclusive language in our liturgical and theological talk. Even though the issue of gender-biased language arose as a theological, liturgical, and ethical issue half a century ago, the church's language concerning God and, to a lesser extent, humanity continues to be patriarchal. The church too often speaks of "men" and "mankind" as terms for all of humanity, reserving "woman" and "womankind" only for females. The implication is that men are the norm of humankind. Likewise, male-dominant language is used to name God. Not only are traditional male terms such as Father, Son, King, and Lord used for the first and second persons of the Trinity, so are male pronouns. It is idolatrous to reduce God to a male image. Moreover, the use of male language for God implies males are made more in the image of God than women. Such a view justifies and perpetuates patriarchy in culture and the church.

The church, then, needs to embrace gender-inclusive language in describing humanity and God in the church. Use of gender-biased language is a long-assimilated habit by church-goers, so preachers should approach the topic pastorally as well as prophetically. We need not beat our parishioners over the head with the call to use inclusive language. On the other hand, they can't see the problem and change the way they speak if we never raise the issue. We preachers can begin by modeling the use of inclusive language in our sermons and prayers. Then, we can gently raise the subject in discussions. And finally we can move toward shaping the liturgy and choosing congregational songs that are inclusive.

A third strategy in combatting patriarchy is to distinguish clearly between "sex" and "gender." Even though the terms are often used as synonyms, as technical terms "sex" refers to biological differences (chromosomes, genitalia, hormones, etc.) and "gender" refers to the way cultures assign certain roles and characteristics (feminine versus masculine) to different sexes. The problem of patriarchy, sexism, and misogyny is with gender, not sex. Biologically speaking, it is true to say that women are different than men, but no hierarchy of valuation accompanies sexual differences. Considering maleness to be better than femaleness only comes with the way male-dominated humanity has constructed gender roles. When preachers talk openly about the difference between biological sex and socially constructed gender, congregations can be liberated from viewing gender valuations as created by God.

Moreover, in our current age, the lines between sexual and gender identities is blurring significantly. Younger generations are refusing to view such identity in strictly binary terms. Not only are people expressing a gender identity that contrasts with their sexual identity, they are physically changing their sexual identity, choosing what pronouns they wish to have applied to them, viewing sexual attraction as a spectrum, and the like. Preachers need to reflect these changes in society in our sermons in order to represent and welcome all into the church. This will require, for many of us, conversations with persons in different social locations than our own to understand and appropriately appreciate these shifting sands. Both the listening to others about these matters and our subsequent speaking about them plays a role in dismantling the hold patriarchy continues to have on the world.

Even though the mainline church generally accepts female leadership these days, there still exists sexist divisions of labor in many congregations that reflect sexist divisions of labor in our society. A fourth homiletical strategy to lift up female leadership in the church and the world, then, is to affirm the priesthood of all believers. Every member of the church has an equal share in the ministry of the baptized. Sermons on Christian vocation can remind congregations that God calls every person into ministry, but not all to the same form of ministry. Valuing all forms of Christian service in the world is a way to lift up women as equal to men in following Christ and serving God.

A fifth homiletical strategy is simple. If in worship we want to counter patriarchal views, the congregation needs to see women performing the same liturgical functions as men. In other words, women need to speak from the pulpit, speak from the lectern, stand at the Table, and serve at the font.

To counter sexism in the Trump era, congregations will need to see women preaching, women proclaiming God's vision for the world that counters Trump's vision for women in the world. If the preaching pastor of a congregation is male, he needs to find occasions to invite lay and clergy women to preach. Women need to see role models of their own sex in the pulpit, and men need to be able to see female preachers as role models. I am amazed how many students in seminary to this day still have seen so few women in the pulpit. Often, female students introduce themselves in my introduction to preaching course by saying they have no plans to preach. Instead they plan to serve on a church staff, and they are only in the course because it is required. Sometimes such an introduction expresses a true sense of vocation, but often it's a sign that the student can't imagine herself in the pulpit because she hasn't had female role models there. Often, these students find a sense of fulfillment in preaching they never expected when they preach their required sermons in class, and their self-images are altered. A similar reaction can occur for laywomen when they are exposed to more female voices in the pulpit.

Similar to having women physically in the pulpit, making sure women are present in the sermon as strong characters in our imagery offers a chance to lift up the equality of women in the world and in the church. In terms of a cumulative homiletic, a sixth strategy is for preachers to lift up women who represent a wide variety of roles in society, while avoiding only using imagery of women in roles that reinforce stereotypes: mothers, wives, nurses, teachers, housewives, and secretaries. Those images are fine—when *mixed* with images of men in similar familial and professional roles and with images of women in a range of other roles— doctor, businesswoman, engineer, probation officer, graduate student, mayor, clergy, and so forth.

In addition to using imagery that shows women are equal to men, preachers need to use imagery of women in a way that asks *all* members of the congregation—female and male—to identify with the women. The more men identify with women in sermons, the less we will see maleness as the norm and femaleness as derivative.

Combined with thinking about how we use women in our sermons, a seventh strategy for combatting sexism and patriarchy is to deal with the presentation of women in the Bible. Preachers must be honest that, as a set of ancient texts, the Christian Bible (including both testaments) is patriarchal in its outlook. One can love scripture and still be honest about problems in it. Indeed, such love requires honesty.

By naming patriarchal elements of a text in a sermon, preachers teach a congregation skills in identifying sexism in other forms of discourse as well, and preachers liberate congregations from the patriarchy we have inherited from scripture. Simply helping a congregation note how rarely women appear in biblical texts, especially as positive or main characters, and how often—when they do appear—they are silenced by male characters and/or the narrator, will be a revelation to some hearers. Identifying such a problem in the text need not take the whole of a sermon but serve as *part* of the "itch" of the sermon to set up good news to follow.

Conversely, preachers need to be intentional about seeking out and lifting up female characters or female imagery in the text when they do appear. While the Bible is overwhelmingly patriarchal, there are individual texts in which that very patriarchy is countered. Indeed, asking a congregation to identify with the female character instead of a male character in a text intuitively leads the hearers to view femaleness as worthy of being honored and considered as a role model for all.

Consider the woman in Mark 5:25–34 with the hemorrhage who comes to Jesus for healing as an example. On the one hand, she appears as a weak character. Not only is she terribly ill, but the narrator gives her no lines to speak to others (she only speaks to herself in v. 28). She is, as women were expected to be in the ancient world, silent in the presence of men. Yet, she is a figure to be admired.

She refuses to accept her state of suffering and reaches out and grabs the salvation she needs to be whole by touching a man known as a healer. And as opposed to chastising her for crossing over cultural boundaries, Jesus calls her action "faith." A preacher can use a story such as this to illustrate overcoming sexism without it consuming the whole sermon, inviting males and females in the congregation to identify with the woman and be invited to participate in breaking down barriers that oppress others themselves.

The grotesque and misogynistic manner in which Donald Trump speaks of and treats women is a painful gift to the church to take up the issue of patriarchy in the wider world and in the church. Preachers cannot be silent and expect their congregations to condemn such attitudes and behavior on their own. A pastor tells of a women's Bible study focused on Genesis 1. When the group read verse 26a, "Let us make humankind in our image, according to our likeness," the pastor asked in what way we are made in God's image. The room was silent. She asked again. Finally, the silence was broken when a woman referred to Genesis 2:18–24 and said, "We are made from the rib of a man. So our husbands are made in God's image, but we are only made in the image of our husbands." Much has been done in recent years to counter such bad and harmful theology, but the Trump era promises to give such thinking prominence again. Preachers can do something about that if they so choose.

CHAPTER 9

LGBT Issues

In spite of Trump holding up a rainbow flag at one of his rallies and mentioning LGBTQ rights in a positive tone, his presidency is positioned to do damage to the rights gained by the LGBTQ community in recent years. This is due to his choice of Mike Pence as his vice president, and his appointment of Kellyanne Conway and Steve Bannon as White House advisors, and Jeff Sessions as Attorney General.

- Jeff Sessions, serving as Alabama attorney general, attempted to prevent a gay rights group from holding a conference at the University of Alabama (1998).[1]

- During his run for Congress, Pence supported the use of federal funds for "conversion therapy" to change a person's sexual orientation from gay to straight (2000).[2]

- Conway complained that the PBS cartoon *Postcards from Buster* included a lesbian couple. She said that parents "don't want their kids looking at a cartoon with a bunch of lesbian mothers" and "regular Americans are standing up and saying... 'I try to protect my kids from outside, external influences corrupting their minds and bodies'" (2005).[3]

- Pence and Sessions supported bills defining marriage as between a man and a woman, saying that prohibiting gay couples from marrying was not discrimination but an enforcement of "God's idea" (2006).[4]

- Pence and Sessions voted against bills banning discrimination on the basis of sexual orientation (2007).

- Pence and Sessions objected to the repeal of "Don't Ask, Don't Tell" in the military (2010).

- Bannon described progressive women as "a bunch of dy**s that came from the Seven Sisters schools up in New England" (2011).[5]

- In an interview with *The New York Times,* Donald Trump explained his stance on gay marriage: "It's like in golf. A lot of people—I don't want this to sound trivial—but a lot of people are switching to these really long putters, very unattractive. It's weird. You see these great players with these really long putters, because they can't sink three-footers anymore. And I hate it. I am a traditionalist. I have so many fabulous friends who happen to be gay, but I am a traditionalist" (2011).[6]

- Conway served as a pollster for the National Organization of Marriage (2012).[7]

- In one of his sexist Twitter attacks on Arianna Huffington, Trump also insulted being gay: "@ ariannahuff is unattractive both inside and out. I fully understand why her former husband left her for a man—he made a good decision" (2014).[8]

- Conway participated in a panel at the Values Voter Summit praising values voters and libertarians as rejecting attempts to "redefine" family to be "whatever feels cool" (2014).[9]

- In a *Fox and Friends* phone interview after Michael Sam was chosen for the NFL draft and kissed his boyfriend, Trump commented, "We've become so politically correct in this country that the country is going to hell—people are afraid to talk. They're afraid to express their own thoughts... I've heard many people, I'm not even speaking for myself, but I've heard many people that thought the display after he was chosen was inappropriate. And whether or not it was, I don't know. But it was certainly out there a little bit" (2014).[10]

- While Bannon was chairman of Breitbart News, numerous anti-LGBT stories were run. Some examples include "Gay Rights Have Made Us Dumber, It's Time to Get Back in the Closet"; "Kids Raised by Same-Sex Couples Twice as Likely to Be Depressed, Fat Adults"; "Day of Silence: How the LGBT Agenda Is Hijacking America's Youth"; and "In Wake of Chattanooga Terror Attack, Provocative Gay Hate-Flag Must Come Down" (2015–16).[11]

- As governor of Indiana, Pence signed the Religious Freedom Restoration Act, which allowed (even though specifically unnamed) for businesses to refuse to provide service to members of the LGBTQ community on religious grounds (Mar. 26, 2015). Only under pressure from state businesses did he sign an amendment to the law prohibiting discrimination against LGBT people (Apr. 2, 2015).

- Trump promised to repeal Obamacare, which prohibits discrimination against transgender persons in accessing health care (Apr. 8, 2015).[12]

- On *Fox News Sunday,* Trump said he would consider appointing Supreme Court justices who would reverse the Court's earlier stance on marriage equality (Jan. 31, 2016).[13]

- Trump initially criticized North Carolina's HB 2, which forces people to use the restrooms assigned to the sex listed on their birth certificate. Within hours, however, he backtracked, asserting states have the right to decide how they see fit concerning the rights of transgendered persons (Apr. 22, 2016). Later in an interview with *The News and Observer* Trump was more explicit, saying, "The state, they know what's going on, they see what's happening, and generally speaking I'm with the state on things like this," he said. "I've spoken with your governor; I've spoken with a lot of different people; and I'm going with the state" (July 6, 2016).[14]

- Bannon commented on Target's bathroom policy, saying the department store is "trying to exclude people who are decent, hard-working people who don't want their four-year-old daughter to have to go into a bathroom with a guy with a beard in a dress" (May 2, 2016).[15]

- Pence criticized the Obama administration's directive concerning transgender restroom access in public schools (May 13, 2016).[16]

- Trump promises to sign the First Amendment Defense Act co-sponsored by Sessions, a federal religious liberties bill allowing for discrimination against LGBTs, if passed by Congress (Sept. 26, 2016).

- The Log Cabin Republicans, an influential LGBT Republican group, refused to endorse Trump after he won the Republican nomination. While they recognized him as "perhaps the most pro-LGBT presidential nominee in the history of the Republican party," they explained their refusal in the following by saying, "As Mr. Trump spoke positively about the LGBT community in the United States, he concurrently surrounded himself with senior advisers with a record of opposing LGBT equality, and committed himself to supporting legislation such as the so-called 'First Amendment Defense Act' that Log Cabin Republicans oppose" (Oct. 22, 2016).[17]

Getting a Handle on the Church's Heterosexism

Human societies have always held a heteronormative worldview in the sense that they have assumed heterosexuality is the norm and homosexuality deviates from the norm. Discrimination against homosexuals was justified in older days on the basis of moral arguments that were some variation of the following: homosexual behavior goes against natural law set forth by God, in which the function of sex is for reproduction of the species. With the advent of psychological studies in the modern era, discrimination against homosexuality has been based as well on the view that homosexuality is an illness.

With the sexual revolution of the 1960s, however, the way Western society viewed homosexuality began to evolve. Medical associations have rejected the idea that homosexuality is deviant behavior or an illness. Over time, being gay came, indeed, not to be seen as a choice but simply as one's sexual orientation (in the same way heterosexuals don't choose to be attracted to the opposite sex but simply are). Indeed, society has slowly come to see sexual attraction and, with it, gender identity as existing on more of spectrum than a clear choice between straight or gay, female or male.

Even with these changes, American heteronormative culture has been slow to protect the rights of gay couples and individuals. Attempts to keep cultural values from changing were numerous and strong. But societal and legal views would change quickly once they began to shift significantly. In 2004, George W. Bush was re-elected in part because conservatives came out to vote for traditional definitions of marriage in numerous state elections.[18] By the next election cycle in 2008, the tide had turned significantly; and during Obama's eight years in office, we have seen the repeal of "Don't Ask, Don't Tell" (2011), numerous states allowing gay marriage (either by legislation or court rulings), the Supreme Court striking down the Defense of Marriage Act and California's Proposition 8 (2013), and the Supreme Court ruling that state-level bans on same-sex marriages are unconstitutional (2015)—in essence extending the legal right to all gay couples across the country. Still, laws that protect people from discrimination in housing, employment, and the like, on the basis of sex, race, or religion, often do not extend to sexual orientation or gender identity.

Along with issues of sexual orientation, cultural views of sexual/gender identity have also evolved even while still being contested. American society is moving toward accepting and protecting the rights of transgender persons. "Transgender" is an umbrella term for persons whose gender identity, gender expression, or behavior does not conform to that typically associated with the sex to which they were assigned at birth. "Transsexual" is a more narrow term referring to a transgender person who seeks to transition or has transitioned to the other physical sex through hormone therapy and/or reassignment surgery changing their sexual anatomy to align with their gender identity. While many continue to see gender expression that differs from one's birth sex as immoral or illogical (e.g., Ben Carson's claim that "choosing" to change one's gender identity is like choosing to change one's ethnicity[19]), psychiatric, psychological, and medical associations now recognize the appropriateness of assisting persons in bringing their bodies in line with their internal gender identity.

While the church has historically been heteronormative in its approach to sexual issues, its recent history in dealing with homosexuality has been mixed. Since the 1960s movements in different denominations have fought for full inclusion of homosexuals in the membership, leadership, and rituals of the church. The Roman Catholic Church and evangelical traditions remain opposed to homosexuality. The Metropolitan Community Church was formed as an inclusive denomination. Mainline denominations have been moving toward inclusion, with the United Church of Christ, the Episcopal Church, the Evangelical Lutheran Church, the Presbyterian Church (USA), and the Christian Church (Disciples of Christ) adopting positions that allow for gay members to be ordained and married. The largest mainline denomination, my own United Methodist Church, continues to fight over the issue, and a split in the coming years may be inevitable if a resolution cannot be found between the evangelical and progressive ends of the denomination. (I've come to recognize that the divide in the church mirrors the divide in the country/culture we have seen in the election and which will likely increase during the Trump presidency.)

Denominational views concerning transgender persons are mixed in a similar fashion as those concerning homosexuality. Perhaps because the Bible has no specific texts mentioning issues related to being transgender and/or because churches have distinguished the issues of gender identity and sexual orientation, some traditions that view homosexuality as a sin have more progressive views concerning transgender issues.

Preaching about Heterosexism

Given the progress in society in legalizing gay marriage and the like, preachers (especially those in denominations that are accepting of gay, bisexual, and transgender people) may have felt that the need to preach about issues of sexual orientation and gender identity has passed. The fact that Donald Trump has filled some of the top ranks of his administration with people who have expressed such strong heterosexist and homophobic views as illustrated above indicates that preachers must continue to be vigilant in protecting those who are vulnerable in our society.

A place to start is for preachers to help hetero-majority congregations understand the terminology used in discussing sexual orientation and gender identity. Many straight and cisgender people (persons who gender identity corresponds with their birth sex) in our pews have primarily heard such terminology used in slang or by the media in ways that are demeaning to the persons to whom they refer or are simply used in ways that lack nuance. When Emily Askew and I began working on *Beyond Heterosexism in the Pulpit*[20] (from which much of the material in this section is drawn), we realized that we struggled with using language precisely even though she (as a lesbian) and I (as an ally) cared about these issues very much. So the first thing we did was to create a glossary of terms for preachers that not only defined terms but warned against the use of some in the pulpit. Providing people in the pews with a proper working vocabulary around these issues will go a long way toward elevating the congregation's conversation concerning these issues. As with most of the homiletical strategies in this book, this one will require of the preacher a cumulative approach. Defining a term once will have only a small impact on hearers. We learn vocabulary through repeated use.

A second homiletical strategy concerns the use of scripture. Preachers certainly need to address the passages that seem to deal with homosexuality (e.g., Gen. 19:1–13; Lev. 18;22; 20:13; Rom. 1:26–27; 1 Cor. 6:9; 1 Tim. 1:9–11). I say, "seem to deal with homosexuality," because scholars interpret some of these texts in different ways when they are viewed in their sociohistorical context than the way they are often used as proof texts. Preachers need to offer these scholarly interpretations to their congregations to help them evaluate the texts in a more critical fashion.

More importantly, though, preachers need to show how other passages and themes of scripture help us reflect on homosexuality in a positive light. There are more than 31,000 verses in the Bible. To only deal with homosexuality in relation to the view of a few verses usually used as part of gay bashing is to let the heterosexists define the terms of the conversation. Any place in scripture in which an author honors or celebrates love between humans can be used to lift up healthy, empowering love between different people today, *including* same sex relationships. When we quit imagining God as obsessed with sex and instead view God as obsessed with love (since God's unconditional love for humanity is such a dominant theme in scripture—*and,* the underlying ethic for all of scripture's commands is "to love our neighbor"), straight people can think about homosexuality more in terms of love than sex.

Similarly, preachers shouldn't only talk about transgender issues in relation to a text such as Deuteronomy 22:5: "A woman shall not wear a man's apparel, nor shall a man put on a woman's garment; for whoever does such things is abhorrent to the Lord your God." Understanding ancient gender bias expressed in this text dealing with cross-dressing might be helpful in a congregation thinking about the role of the Bible in dealing with complex contemporary issues, but, in truth, the Bible nowhere deals with what we mean today by "transgender" or "transsexual." Texts that help congregations reflect on the way we are all created in God's image and all are created good would be a better starting point.

In truth, scripture can only be so helpful in preaching about sexual orientation and gender identity, because the divide between ancient and contemporary understanding of these issues is so wide. A third homiletic strategy, then, is for the preacher to draw on contemporary reason and experience as theological authorities over against scripture and tradition when dealing with these matters. While preachers should beware of sounding like a medical journal, they should not fear bringing in contemporary scientific concepts related to homosexual, bisexual, transgender, and transsexual issues. More important is experience. Preachers need to put a face on the issues being discussed. When straight, cisgender preachers share experiences of gay and transgender persons in sermon images, congregations will be invited to move beyond thinking about the issues in the abstract and instead think about them in relation to real people's lives. Indeed, moving beyond the sharing of others' experiences, preachers would do well to invite people of different sexual orientations and different gender identities to share their own stories personally if a congregation would be hospitable to them. If gay or transgender persons share their stories as part of the proclamation of the gospel—that is, as a personal testimony celebrating God's grace and care for the person—congregations can be led to join in that celebration.

In addition to using the experiences of gay and transgender persons to talk about issues of sexual orientation and gender identity, a fourth homiletical strategy involves using the experiences of such people in sermon imagery about topics unrelated to sexuality and gender. Such a strategy can be helpful in normalizing homosexual and transgender persons for straight, cisgender hearers. Congregations can come to see them as people instead of only as gay or transgender people: a transwoman who is a model of philanthropy, a gay couple caught in the web of materialism; an older gay man struggling with arthritis. In other words, we need to be at ease with speaking about and helping the congregation be at ease hearing about gay people simply as people. In our stories, we need to use homosexual characters with whom we want everyone in the pews (regardless of their sexual orientation) to identify. In sum, we need to use gay and transgender people in our sermons as representative humans instead of only as representative homosexual and transgender persons. (As we named in the chapter on race, straight, cisgender preachers must be careful not to tokenize persons of different sexual orientations and gender identities in the process of lifting them up in this manner. For example, one does better to tell a story about Lynn and mention in passing her partner Rachel, not, "Lynn, a lesbian woman...")

A final homiletical strategy is broader than the first four. Preachers need to talk about sexual ethics frankly. The only time many preachers seem to mention sex is in relation to homosexuality. Preachers can offer congregations a sexual ethic that involves discussions of love, commitment, consent, and marriage apart from specifically discussing straight or gay relationships—that is, a sexual ethics discussion that applies to gay *and* straight people. Surely, then, congregations can recognize that a committed, gay relationship is considerably more ethical than the sexual ethic Donald Trump promotes in the way he speaks of sexual conquests, prenuptial agreements, groping women because he is a celebrity, and the like.

Rights gained by gay and transgender Americans in recent years are at risk under Trump's administration. While it is unclear whether Trump himself has an explicit agenda in relation to these rights, it is absolutely clear that some members of his administration do. Preachers cannot assume that the progress made will continue. We must be vigilant in advocating for a just society on the basis of God's vision for the world for people regardless of gender identity or sexual orientation, and in shaping the church as a community hospitable to all seeking to follow Jesus Christ regardless of sexual orientation or gender identity.

CHAPTER 10

Islam

Many of the lines below were repeated by Trump and his team numerous times:

- Trump said, "I didn't see Swedish people knocking down the Trade Center" (Apr. 2011).[1]

- While Steve Bannon was CEO, *Breitbart* made Pamela Geller, who sponsored contests for drawing cartoons of Muhammad, and Frank Gaffney, a Muslim conspiracy theorist, columnists. During Bannon's time, *Breitbart* ran Islamophobic stories such as, "Political Correctness Protects Muslim Rape Culture," "6 Reasons Pamela Geller's Muhammad Cartoon Contest Is No Different from Selma," and, "How Muslim Migrants Devastate a Community" (2015).[2]

- At a Trump town hall meeting, an attendee asserted that Obama is a Muslim (a statement Trump did not correct) and asked how Trump planned to get rid of Muslim training camps in the country. Trump responded, "We're going to be looking at a lot of different things. You know, a lot of people are saying that and a lot of people are saying bad things are happening" (Sept. 17, 2015).[3]

- In an interview on *Meet the Press* following the above incident, Ben Carson (now Trump's nominee to head the Department of Housing and Urban Development) was asked whether the president's faith should matter. He said, "I guess it depends on what that faith is... If it's inconsistent with the values and principles of America, then of course it should matter, but if it fits within the realm of America and consistent with the constitution, no problem." In answer to a follow-up question about a Muslim being president, he said, "No, I would not advocate that we put a Muslim in charge of this nation. I absolutely would not agree with that." He went on to claim that Islam is not compatible with the Constitution (September 20, 2015).[4]

- In a *Fox Business* interview, Trump advocated monitoring mosques and, when asked if he would consider closing mosques, he responded, "Absolutely, I think it's great" (Oct. 29, 2015).[5]

- When Yahoo News asked if Trump planned to register Muslims in a database or give them a form of special identification noting their religion, Trump refused to reject the idea, saying, "We're going to have to look at a lot of things very closely. We're going to have to look at mosques" (Nov. 19, 2015).[6] Later, during questions at campaign stops, Trump affirmed his White House would "absolutely" implement a database that tracks Muslims in the country and that it would require "good management" to get all Muslims registered. When asked later what difference there was between his Muslim registration plan and the Nazis' policy requiring all Jews to register, he only said, "You tell me" (Nov. 18, 2015).[7]

- Trump claimed to have seen "thousands and thousands" of Muslims celebrating the terrorist attack on September 11, 2001. There is no evidence such an event took place (Nov. 22, 2015).[8]

- Days after the shooting in San Bernardino, Trump issued a policy proposal calling for "a complete and total shutdown of Muslims entering the United States until our country's representatives can figure out what the hell is going on." Part of his rationale for the ban was that "there is a great hatred towards Americans by large segments of the Muslim population" (Dec. 7, 2015).[9]

- When asked, "Is it a Muslim problem or a radical Islamist problem?" Trump responded, "Maybe it's a Muslim problem, maybe not" (Feb. 4, 2016).[10]

- When Trump was asked during a debate, "Last night on CNN you said, 'Islam hates us.' Did you mean all 1.6 billion Muslims?" Trump began his answer, "I mean a lot of 'em"   (Mar. 9, 2016).[11]

- The day after the Pulse Nightclub shooting, Trump stated that the U.S should suspend immigration from areas of the world where there is a history of terrorism against the United States, Europe, or U.S. allies until the U.S. fully understands how to end these threats. In a follow-up tweet, Trump advocated, "suspending immigration from nations tied to Islamic terror" (June 13, 2016).[12]

- During a town hall debate, a Muslim American asked Trump how he would "help people like me deal with the consequences of being labeled as a threat to the country after the election is over." Trump responded, "You're right about Islamophobia and that's a shame. But one thing we have to do is we have to make sure that, because there is a problem, I mean whether we like it or not and we can be politically correct but whether we like it or not there is a problem. And we have to be sure that Muslims come in and report when they see something going on, when they see hatred going on they have to report it. As an example, in San Bernardino many people saw the bombs all over the apartment of the two people that killed fourteen and wounded many, many people—horribly wounded, they'll never be the same... [The claim that others saw the couple's weapons has been disproven.] These are radical Islamic terrorists and she [Clinton] won't even mention the word..." (Oct. 9, 2016).[13]

• Carl Higbie, a Trump surrogate during the campaign, cited the Japanese Internment Camps during World War II as "precedent" for registering Muslim Immigrants (Nov. 17, 2016).[14]

Getting a Handle on the Church's Islamophobia

In light of his focus on terrorist mass shootings in the United States, it is striking how much emphasis Donald Trump has put on the Second Amendment protection of the right to bear arms and so little on the emphasis on the First Amendment's protection for the freedom of religion—well, at least religions he doesn't like. He is willing to sign into law a bill supporting religious liberty for Christians[15] (that is, to protect Christian business from having to serve LGBT patrons) but unwilling to protect Muslims from discrimination, even to the point of his proposing a ban on all Muslims from entering the United States and a forced registration of Muslims in the States.

Trump's position may be striking, but it is not surprising. The U.S. has a history of oppression of Muslims. Indeed, it is estimated that 10–15 percent of slaves brought over from Africa were Muslim, but practice of Islam was banned by slave owners, with most Muslims being forced to convert to Christianity. Then, immigration from the Middle East brought Muslims to the Midwest during the sixty years following the

Civil War. Many of these people ended up working in the hot, dire conditions of the Ford Motor Company's assembly lines. Immigration restrictions, however, followed for thirty years, keeping the number of Muslim immigrants relatively small; but, with Black migration from southern states to the North, many African Americans converted to Islam. There were 1000 mosques in the U.S. in 1952 when immigration restrictions were lightened and a new influx of Muslims came to the States.[16] Today, Islam is the third largest religion in the United States, comprising just under one percent of the population (following Christianity and Judaism).[17] As Muslim numbers continue to grow (along with other factors), Christians feel their hold on the U.S. as a supposedly "Christian society" slipping further and further away, and the church (and Christians running the country) become more defensive.

While Christian Americans were quite willing to look down on Muslims before 9/11, the attack that day gave many a sense of justification to stereotype and discriminate against Islam and those who practice it. When grief, anger, and fear are mixed together, poured into a dish composed of civil religion, and baked at 350 degrees for fifteen years, the result is a casserole of arrogant hatred.

Indeed, hate crimes against Muslims have been on the rise since 2001; and, likely inspired by the Islamophobic rhetoric of the primary season, such crimes against Muslims and Arabs were up 78 percent in 2015 over 2014.[18] (Statistics for 2016 are not yet available.) One wonders how many of these acts of violence have been perpetuated in the name of Jesus Christ.

While the church has flourished under American freedom of religion, we have been far too willing to have the state infringe on the freedom and rights of non-Christians. Too often, Christian congregations fight against Muslims building a mosque or community center in their city. Too often, we allow an equation between Muslims (generally) and Muslim terrorists to go unchallenged. Indeed, we are all too happy to quote Jesus saying, "I am the way" (Jn. 14:6), while ignoring him saying, "I have other sheep that do not belong to this fold" (Jn. 10:16).

Preaching about Islamophobia

Before offering specific strategies for bringing Islam and Muslims into sermons, we should name how odd it is to promote the idea of speaking about another religion as part of Christian worship, unless it is part of an apologetic move in defending Christianity against the other religion. The very purpose of Christian preaching is to interpret and offer beliefs and practices of Christian faith to those in attendance. Doesn't speaking positively about another religion undermine Christian preaching?

No, not when we see the issue in the proper perspective. Central to Christian faith are ethics—and the core Christian ethic is to love our neighbors as ourselves. One cannot love a neighbor when one holds a distorted image of that neighbor. We preach about Islam to combat Islamophobia, as part of the church's continual efforts to love our neighbors more fully.

A beginning point, then, for helping people in the pews shift away from stereotypes of Muslims/Islam and conflating Islam with terrorism is to be honest about the church's history and stereotypes. Today's church is stereotyped by the most pubic of evangelicals involved in televangelism and political activism. Without in any way denying these people's right to their public speech, many Christians feel the media and wider public too often lump us all together as if we agree with whatever they say. When James Dobson, Franklin Graham, Jerry Falwell Jr., or the like express a far-right opinion, too often it is considered the "Christian viewpoint" on the matter—even though millions of conservative, moderate, and progressive Christians may disagree.

Worse, we have had plenty of times throughout history during which elements of the church radicalized and became violent. After Constantine legalized Christianity, some Christians shifted from being persecuted to persecuting others. The Crusades used theological rationales to support many a war crime (even to the point of sending children into battle to help expel Muslims from the Holy Land) that resulted in lining the pockets of European land holders and political figures. The church in the southern U.S. supported the enslavement of people of African descent. Even Nazism in early and mid-twentieth century Germany considered itself a Christian movement. We could add in fringe distortions of Christianity such as the Ku Klux Klan, Peoples Temple, Branch Davidians, and the Alt-right.

Because Western culture has, for the most part, been a Christian culture and has controlled the narrative of history in the West, these types of events and groups are portrayed as exceptions to the rule, as unsightly scars on our identity and purpose. Were we only one percent of the population, however, the story might be told in such a way that the people and incidents mentioned above might well be at the center of how the world names us. If we name this reality in the pulpit and confess our willingness to view over 20 percent of the world's population (second only to Christianity, at around 30 percent of the world's population) in relation to stereotypes and the horrific actions of a miniscule percentage of adherents of Islam, those in the pew might be more open to viewing Muslims as they wish to be known instead of viewing the whole of a religion based on its fringe elements. It's sort of a "do-unto-others…" thing. Indeed, we might even move to the point of empathizing with Muslims who suffer because of the reputations they don't deserve and because, far more often than we, *they* are the victims of terrorism.

With such empathy established, preachers can employ a second strategy of reminding the church that we are called to care for the orphan, widow, and the sojourner. Any time a biblical text used in a sermon deals with such topics, the preacher can appropriately bring Muslim refugees into the sermon. The refugee crisis in the world today is an immense tragedy. There are many times the church would have been talking about and responding to this in significant ways. Because of our current fear of terrorism, however, our response has been slow and small, betraying who we are as the body of Christ. People in the church can have differing opinions about how best to vet immigrants, while still being embarrassed at how few Syrian refugees the U.S. has accepted and advocating for getting processes in place quickly, so those seeking asylum can find it in our country with the church's assistance.

Another strategy for preachers to consider in combatting inappropriate and oppressive stereotypes is to help congregations actually understand something of the character, belief, and practices of Islam. A first step in this strategy involves helping Christians develop a more respectful view of other religions in general. Respect doesn't require agreement. We can disagree with the beliefs of other religions and still recognize (1) the people practicing those religions are as honest and sincere in their quest to be in relationship with and serve the Divine as are we, and (2) God, whom we hold to be all-loving, is mysterious enough to relate to other peoples in whatever ways God chooses, relieving us of any responsibility to judge them.

Holding such a stance does not mean the church relinquishes its call to evangelism. We still can (and should!) share our story with anyone who will listen. However, sharing our story is not the same as saying, "Take it or leave it." We faithfully share the good news of Jesus Christ, and trust God with whatever follows.

A second step in this strategy is developing an added appreciation specifically for the other Abrahamic religions. To recognize a common heritage with Judaism and Islam doesn't require Christianity to relinquish its uniqueness.

Yet it does allow us to celebrate a connection found in Ancestry.com with these two religions that we do not have with other religions such as Hinduism, Taoism, or Confucianism. There is shared story in our background that invites conversation between Christianity, Judaism, and Islam. Preachers should look for occasions to focus on the Abrahamic narrative and name the shared lineage appreciatively, especially in texts that reference Hagar as mother of the Arabs. The connection with Islam (and Judaism) need not be the focus of the sermon for the preacher to highlight it in passing. Such repeated, occasional references will go a long way to normalizing the church's view of its distant cousin, Islam.

A third step of this strategy involves the preacher finding ways to teach the congregation about some of the basics of Islam. The goal of such teaching is not to promote Islam, but to remove the stigma we assign to it. Preachers can highlight similarities we have with Islam—such as monotheism, an emphasis on prayer and fasting, and an appreciation of Jesus—while also naming differences—such as the very different understandings of Jesus, the role of Muhammad, the Qur'an, etc. Also, though, just naming Islam on its own terms (that is, without referring to Christianity) will go a long way toward understanding our Muslim neighbors and toward Christians better understanding references to Islam they see in the news. For instance, preachers can describe the Five Pillars of Islam: recitation of the testimony of faith ("There is no God but Allah, and Muhammad is the Messenger of God."); performing ritual prayers five times a day; almsgiving; fasting during Ramadan; and pilgrimage to Mecca. By respecting the devotion of Muslims, Christians will be in a better place to defend the rights of Muslims in the public sphere. When pastors have not studied Islam on their own, they can invite Muslim leaders to visit worship (or another ecclesial setting) to explain the tenets of Islam on their own terms. Having a person being open and nondefensive about

questions from Christians can go a long way toward breaking
down stereotypes of Muslims.

———————————

I was serving as Dean of the Chapel at DePauw University
in Greencastle, Indiana, when the terrorist attack on 9/11
took place. That small, conservative Midwestern town could
have easily been a place where anti-Muslim sentiment
became very strong, very quickly. But on the evening of
September 11, the town held a prayer vigil. Every pastor in
town and every religious group on campus was invited to say
a word and lead a prayer. Significantly different theological
perspectives were on parade. One of those was offered by
the Muslim Student Association and their faculty advisor.
Because they wept over their country being under attack,
and because they prayed for God's healing and protection
of us all, the people of Greencastle didn't turn their fear of
terrorism into hatred of Muslims. The dominantly Christian
gathering was able to distinguish the sincere religious
endeavor of Islam (even if they disagreed with it) from
the hate-filled and destruction-oriented acts of terrorists. I
suspect the Muslim faculty and students who stood before
that crowd had second thoughts. They had experienced
discrimination in the past and it could have gotten worse
at that point. But their vulnerability brought out the best in
the church that night.

I left DePauw many years ago, but I have often thought
of that night in the midst of the 2015–16 campaign cycle.
I wonder what the tiny Muslim community at DePauw
thinks of entering into a time when Trump will be their
president and may deny their patriotism. I wonder how
they have fared in Greencastle during the election cycle. Has
Greencastle continued to be a hospitable home for them?
Have churches continued to pray with and for them? Have
preachers welcomed them into their community as guests

and proclaimed their worth in God's eyes—worth the church must continue to name before the new, Trumpian powers-that-be? I hope so. And I hope the work of those small churches and their preachers is contagious, spreading across my land and your land...and their land...as Christians claim religious liberty and respect for our Abrahamic brothers and sisters who are American Muslims, Muslim immigrants, and Muslim refugees.

EPILOGUE

It was November 9, 2016. Election day. My daughter was a week shy of being eighteen, a week shy of being able to vote. Yet this was for her in many ways her first election. She had been engaged in the primary and general election process for the previous year and a half in ways she hadn't been four years earlier. Maggie, like so many (especially women and girls) was excited at the possibility of the United States having its first woman president. Were Hillary Clinton to have been elected, Maggie would have seen her future open in ways it seems less to now. However, her desire to see a woman in the Oval Office instead of only in the Office of the First Lady wasn't all that grabbed her attention during this election. As a late-teenager, her passion for social policy and even international affairs was beginning to blossom. I say all of this out of a sense of pride, but also to set the final stage for this book.

It was November 9, 2016. Election day. Instead of watching the results with my wife and me in the family room, Maggie threw an election party so she and other high school-aged friends could celebrate together in the basement. She decorated the room with streamers. She had paper plates and plastic cups. It was all in blue. No red to be seen. By the end of the evening, however, my daughter and her friends themselves were pretty blue.

In fact, Maggie and her friends were crushed. They couldn't believe the country that they were on their way to loving as engaged adults could elect someone who had expressed such hate during the election. There were tears, and rightfully so. One should grieve at a funeral. An ideal of America died for my daughter that night. In all future elections and political processes, she will be a realist.

Those of us who have lived through numerous elections have a historical perspective about these things. We know there is an ebb and flow to the country's political tastes, especially when it comes to the presidency. We expect the POTUS-pendulum to swing between Republicans and Democrats. We expect some of the candidates to whom we are deeply committed to lose. So when Trump won on November 9, 2016, many of us could say, "This, too, shall pass."

This historical perspective warns against us preachers engaging in some of the hyperbole that has risen up after the election. Granted, the election was defined by hyperbole from the media and spectators (with the election often being called the most important election of modern times) as well as by the candidates themselves. The election of Donald Trump doesn't mean that democracy has come to an end and we've substituted a dictator for a president. In spite of how we feel about the man Donald Trump, we can still hold onto respect and hope for the office of the president in terms of a long-range view of American politics. We can still assume checks and balances built into the system will do their job. "Trump, too, shall pass."

On the other hand, having a historical perspective that keeps us from speaking in hyperbole shouldn't be taken as permission to keep from speaking about Trump and his presidency altogether. As we have seen in the previous chapters, the views of Trump, some of the closest members of his administration, and some of his most avid (rabid?) supports represent very real possibilities of reversing much progress our country has made in respect for the diversity of our population, and very real threats to the well-being of many non-white, non-male, non-Christian, non-citizen, non-cisgender, and non-straight members of our society.

Moreover, in this book, I have only focused on the groups upon whose backs Trump has placed targets. There are many other types of issues with which the church should (must!) be concerned):

1. Trump's flippant manner in talking about war generally, and nuclear armament specifically;

2. his attempts to look as if he is avoiding conflicts between his business interests and his role in government while doing as little as possible (and constantly reminding the public that by law he doesn't have to do anything);

3. his choice of appointees who are rich supporters without any regard for their qualifications for the position they will hold;

4. the hints that the Trump administration is keeping an enemies list;

5. his quick trigger attacks on anyone who challenges him, even to the point of mocking a disabled journalist in the most despicable of manners;

6. his public appreciation for the Philippines' president's violent approach to dealing with drug dealers;

7. his desire to repeal the Affordable Care Act, which, despite his protestations otherwise, will likely remove access to healthcare for the nation's poor;

8. his lack of concern for honesty or consistency regarding things he has said in the past;

9. his reluctance to have security briefings and to accept what they say;

10. his bromance with Vladimir Putin;

11. his willingness to use torture in interrogations; and

12. his dismissal of climate change as a "Chinese hoax."

The church will need to be a strong and courageous ethical voice in our country in the coming years.

While Trump, too, will pass, in the four to eight years before he passes out of the White House, he can do significant damage that runs counter to the church's understanding of God's will for the world. We believe the world should be characterized by love of neighbor, while, on New Year's Eve, Trump tweeted a view of his presidency rooted in hatred and domination of enemies: "Happy New Year to all, including to my many enemies and those who have fought me and lost so badly they just don't know what to do. Love." He calls the country (and invites the church to tag along) to be the worst version of ourselves instead of the best we have to offer one another, the world, and God. He is a small man and will likely be a small president.

The church must heed God's call and not let Trump's bigotry and hatred be the loudest voice of the day. This is an opportunity for preachers to claim the mantle that Trump has unintentionally laid on our shoulders and reclaim the pulpit as a place where prophecy is heard.

An acquaintance recounted attending church on Sunday, January 1, New Year's Day. The pastor's sermonic focus was a review of 2016 and looking toward the future. In the entire sermon, though, the preacher never mentioned Donald Trump or the election once! The parishioner was surprised and disappointed. I was disappointed, but I wasn't surprised.

This past September I preached a sermon at Perkins Chapel that dealt with the United Methodist General Conference. At General Conference, we United Methodists fought, once again, over the inclusion of homosexuals in our fold. A denominational split was beginning to look inevitable to many people. I felt that the voices of those who supported the restriction of LGBT persons from the rites and leadership of the church were being heard in my setting far more than those who supported the full inclusion of LGBT persons in the life of the church. The sermon was on Micah

6:1–8, and I spoke of my church as being on trial for failing to do justice in the same way the text viewed ancient Israel as being on trial. I put the current forms of discrimination in the context of past denomination discrimination against women and African Americans.

After the sermon, a new seminarian approached me. He introduced himself and then said that he had grown up in church and never once had he heard any of those issues (racism, sexism, or heterosexism) mentioned in the pulpit. There were tears, and rightfully so. I grieved that the pulpits he sat before for thirty or so years had been so silent, so dead, in relation to such important matters.

We can't let that be the case for any Christian attending church in the next four (or, heaven forbid, eight) years! In the era of Trump, those worshiping as part of the body of Christ must hear voices that counter the hateful, and frankly scary, rhetoric of Trump and his legion. I say without hyperbole: while this may not be the end of our country as we know it, this situation is a serious crisis for the country...and the church. And we need serious preachers offering serious sermons that present different views and hopes for the world than the views that won the election. I pray that the era of Trump leads to a revival of preaching related to social justice themes of God's good news that essentially makes the era of Trump null and void in reshaping the diverse landscape of American society.

NOTES

Chapter 1: Confessing Our Shock and Awe

[1] http://www.nbc.com/saturday-night-live/video/election-night/3424956?snl=1.

Chapter 2: A Postmodern Presidency

[1] For example, O. Wesley Allen Jr., *The Homiletic of All Believers: A Conversational Approach to Proclamation and Preaching* (Louisville: Westminster John Knox Press, 2005); and, coauthored with Ronald J. Allen, *The Sermon without End: A Conversational Approach to Preaching* (Nashville: Abingdon Press, 2015).

[2] Stanley J. Grenz, *A Primer on Postmodernism* (Grand Rapids: Eerdmans, 1996), 43.

[3] For a longer discussion of my approach as a "light postmodernist," see O. Wesley Allen Jr., *Preaching and the Human Condition* (Nashville: Abingdon Press, 2016) 4–6.

[4] https://www.oxforddictionaries.com/press/news/2016/11/17/WOTY-16.

[5] http://www.cc.com/video-clips/63ite2/the-colbert-report-the-word---truthiness.

Chapter 4: Us and Them

[1] The statistic and following quotes can be found on the SPLC's website: https://www.splcenter.org/20161129/ten-days-after-harassment-and-intimidation-aftermath-election. Accessed on December 12, 2016.

Chapter 5: Love Trumps Hate, But Only If We Love Trump

[1] Martin Luther King Jr., *Stride Toward Freedom: The Montgomery Story* (New York: Harper & Row, 1958), 102–3.

[2] Gustavo Gutiérrez, as quoted in John Dear, *The God of Peace: Toward a Theology of Nonviolence* (Maryknoll, N.Y.: Orbis, 1994), 152; taken from Gustavo Gutiérrez, *A Theology of Liberation: History, Politics, and Salvation* (Maryknoll, N.Y.: Orbis, 1973).

[3] For Lowry's discussion of the movement from itch to scratch, see Eugene Lowry, *The Homiletical Plot: The Sermon as Narrative Art Form*,

expanded ed. (Louisville: Westminster John Knox Press, 2001; originally pub. Nashville: Abingdon Press, 1971), 15–21.

⁴ See Michael A. Brothers, *Distance in Preaching: Room to Speak, Room to Listen* (Grand Rapids: Eerdmans, 2014).

⁵ https://www.reddit.com/r/Christianity/comments/5doj33/if_muslims_are_forced_to_register_in_the_us_we/

Chalpter 6: Making the Church Great Again

¹ O. Wesley Allen Jr., *Preaching and the Human Condition: Loving God, Self and Others* (Nashville: Abingdon Press, 2016.

Chapter 7: Race

¹ http://www.nytimes.com/2016/08/28/us/politics/donald-trump-housing-race.html?_r=0.

² http://www.al.com/news/index.ssf/2016/12/civil_rights_activists_1985_vo.html.

³ John O'Donnell, *Trumped! The Inside Story of the Real Donald Trump—His Cunning Rise and Spectacular Fall* (New York: Simon & Schuster, 1991).

⁴ http://www.upi.com/Archives/1992/10/19/Trump-Plaza-loses-appeal-of-discrimination-penalty/1911719467200/.

⁵ http://www.msnbc.com/all-in/watch/trump-in-1993-they-don-t-look-indian-716425283908.

⁶ http://www.cnn.com/2016/09/09/politics/donald-trump-birther/.

⁷ https://www.washingtonpost.com/news/post-politics/wp/2015/06/16/full-text-donald-trump-announces-a-presidential-bid/?utm_term=.db586ba3841b.

⁸ https://www.bostonglobe.com/metro/2015/08/20/after-two-brothers-allegedly-beat-homeless-man-one-them-admiringly-quote-donald-trump-deporting-illegals/I4NXR3Dr7litLi2NB4f9TN/story.html.

⁹ http://www.cbsnews.com/pictures/wild-donald-trump-quotes/11/.

¹⁰ http://www.cnn.com/2015/11/22/politics/donald-trump-black-lives-matter-protester-confrontation/.

¹¹ http://www.politico.com/story/2016/01/trump-neo-nazi-retweet-218113.

¹² https://www.washingtonpost.com/news/fact-checker/wp/2016/03/01/donald-trump-and-david-duke-for-the-record/?utm_term=.0434673bc1e8.

¹³ http://www.wsj.com/articles/donald-trump-keeps-up-attacks-on-judge-gonzalo-curiel-1464911442.

¹⁴ https://www.nytimes.com/2016/11/19/us/politics/trump-university.html.

¹⁵ http://www.politifact.com/truth-o-meter/article/2016/jul/05/donald-trumps-star-david-tweet-recap/.

¹⁶ http://www.cbsnews.com/news/quotes-from-steve-bannon-trumps-new-white-house-chief-strategist/.

¹⁷ http://www.vanityfair.com/news/2016/09/donald-trump-jr-pepe-nazi-instagram.

¹⁸ https://www.washingtonpost.com/news/post-politics/wp/2016/09/20/african-americans-are-in-the-worst-shape-theyve-ever-been-trump-says-in-north-carolina/?utm_term=.068adfe8ccb1.

[19] https://www.washingtonpost.com/opinions/anti-semitism-is-no-longer-an-undertone-of-trumps-campaign-its-the-melody/2016/11/07/b1ad6e22-a50a-11e6-8042-f4d111c862d1_story.html?utm_term=.19fdea7389ad.

[20] http://www.latimes.com/nation/politics/trailguide/la-na-trailguide-updates-neo-nazi-alt-right-crowd-cheers-the-1479774847-htmlstory.html.

[21] http://fortune.com/2016/11/19/jeff-sessions-race-civil-rights/.

[22] http://www.huffingtonpost.com/entry/donald-trump-kkk-parade-north-carolina_us_5844eb97e4b017f37fe5591c.

[23] https://www.washingtonpost.com/news/the-fix/wp/2016/12/21/bill-oreilly-rose-to-the-defense-of-white-privilege-in-americas-presidential-voting-process/?utm_term=.be67485a4b7d.

[24] http://www.nytimes.com/2016/11/20/us/politics/white-nationalists-celebrate-an-awakening-after-donald-trumps-victory.html.

[25] https://www.youtube.com/watch?v=1q881g1L_d8.

[26] http://www.cnn.com/2016/12/22/us/mall-racist-rant-trnd/.

Chapter 8: Gender

[1] The incidents in this bulleted list were compiled by Claire Cohen, http://www.telegraph.co.uk/women/politics/donald-trump-sexism-tracker-every-offensive-comment-in-one-place/. Cohen lists many others that space does not allow us to include here.

[2] http://www.vanityfair.com/news/2016/10/graydon-carter-on-donald-trump.

[3] http://www.telegraph.co.uk/women/politics/donald-trump-sexism-tracker-every-offensive-comment-in-one-place/.

[4] https://en.wikipedia.org/wiki/Donald_Trump_sexual_misconduct_allegations.

[5] http://www.catalyst.org/knowledge/women-sp-500-companies.

[6] http://time.com/money/4207416/hollywood-wage-gap/.

[7] https://www.ncronline.org/news/vatican/pope-francis-confirms-finality-ban-ordaining-women.

Chapter 9: LGBT Issues

[1] http://www.cnn.com/2016/12/01/politics/kfile-jeff-sessions-lgbt-conference/.

[2] http://web.archive.org/web/20010519165033fw_/http://cybertext.net/pence/issues.html.

[3] http://www.mediamatters.org/research/2016/08/17/media-meet-donald-trump-s-new-campaign-manager-kellyanne-conway/212458.

[4] Most of the items concerning Pence in this bulleted list come from Will Drabold's *Time* article collecting Pence's stance over the years; http://time.com/4406337/mike-pence-gay-rights-lgbt-religious-freedom/.

[5] http://www.cbsnews.com/news/quotes-from-steve-bannon-trumps-new-white-house-chief-strategist/.

[6] http://www.cbsnews.com/pictures/wild-donald-trump-quotes/17/.

[7] http://www.nationalreview.com/corner/343896/why-gay-marriage-and-conservatism-are-incompatible-frank-schubert.

[8] https://twitter.com/realdonaldtrump/status/240462265680289792?lang=en.

[9] http://www.rightwingwatch.org/post/maggie-gallagher-warns-of-the-horrible-things-the-left-is-going-to-do-as-they-impose-this-new-strange-sexual-orthodoxy/

[10] http://www.huffingtonpost.com/entry/donald-trump-fox-michael-sam_us_57605239e4b053d43306854a.

[11] https://www.queerty.com/10-antigay-headlines-overseen-trumps-top-advisor-steve-bannon-20161114.

[12] https://theestablishment.co/trumps-health-care-amendments-could-be-deadly-for-trans-people-a513bc3c0efd#.iiducx1by.

[13] http://www.foxnews.com/transcript/2016/01/31/ted-cruz-attacks-donald-trump-financial-record-trump-responds/.

[14] http://www.newsobserver.com/news/politics-government/politics-columns-blogs/under-the-dome/article87997922.html.

[15] https://soundcloud.com/breitbart/breitbart-news-daily-sandy-rios-may-2-2016.

[16] http://fox59.com/2016/05/13/indiana-schools-react-to-obama-administrations-directive-on-transgender-access-to-school-bathrooms/

[17] http://www.cnn.com/2016/10/22/politics/log-cabin-republicans-donald-trump/.

[18] http://www.nbcnews.com/id/6383353/ns/politics/t/voters-pass-all-bans-gay-marriage/#.WHUfPX0gcYs.

[19] http://www.cnn.com/2016/07/19/politics/ben-carson-transgender/.

[20] Emily Askew and O. Wesley Allen Jr., *Beyond Heterosexism in the Pulpit* (Eugene, Oreg.: Cascade, 2015).

Chapter 10: Islam

[1] http://www.newsmax.com/InsideCover/donald-trump-muslim-problem/2011/03/30/id/391238/.

[2] http://www.independent.co.uk/news/people/steve-bannon-breitbart-donald-trumps-chief-strategist-a7416606.html.

[3] http://www.cnn.com/2015/09/17/politics/donald-trump-obama-muslim-new-hampshire/.

[4] http://www.nbcnews.com/meet-the-press/amp/ben-carson-does-not-believe-muslim-should-be-president-n430431?client+safari

[5] http://www.nbcnews.com/politics/2016-election/his-words-donald-trump-muslim-ban-deportations-n599901.

[6] https://www.yahoo.com/news/trump-seeks-to-walk-back-1304338462375990.html.

[7] http://www.nationalreview.com/corner/427418/watch-trumps-exchange-muslims-registering-government-jim-geraghty.

[8] http://www.politifact.com/truth-o-meter/statements/2015/nov/22/donald-trump/fact-checking-trumps-claim-thousands-new-jersey-ch/.

[9] http://www.nbcnews.com/politics/2016-election/trump-calls-complete-shutdown-muslims-entering-u-s-n475821.

[10] https://www.youtube.com/watch?v=RAZi-5Ex7kc.

[11] http://www.cnn.com/2015/12/08/politics/donald-trump-muslims/.

[12] http://www.theatlantic.com/international/archive/2016/06/trump-muslims-ban-orlando/486950/.

[13] https://thinkprogress.org/trump-debate-islamophobia-42e7fce28a71#.itfhn57ca.

[14] https://www.washingtonpost.com/news/morning-mix/wp/2016/11/17/japanese-internment-is-precedent-for-national-muslim-registry-prominent-trump-backer-says/?tid=a_inl&utm_term=.961c645501d1.

[15] http://www.nationalreview.com/article/440502/trump-supports-bill-protecting-religious-liberty-introduced-mike-lee.

[16] http://www.pbs.org/opb/historydetectives/feature/islam-in-america/.

[17] http://www.pewforum.org/religious-landscape-study/.

[18] https://www.documentcloud.org/documents/3110202-SPECIAL-STATUS-REPORT-v5-9-16-16.html.

CPSIA information can be obtained
at www.ICGtesting.com
Printed in the USA
FSOW03n2017060417

9 780827 231481